SICILY

By the staff of Editions Berlitz

Preface

A new kind of travel guide for the jet age—and one of an extensive series by Berlitz on the world's top tourist areas—this compact and colourful book is packed with all you need to know about Sicily.

Like our phrase books and dictionaries, this book fits your pocket—in both size and price. It also aims to fit your travel needs:

- It concentrates on your specific destination—Sicily—not an entire country.

- It combines easy reading with fast facts: what to see and do, where to shop, what to eat.

- An authoritative A-to-Z "blueprint" fills the back of the book, giving clear-cut answers to all your questions, from "How do I get from the airport into town?" to "Can I drink the water?"—plus how to get there, when to go and what to budget.

- Easy-to-read, full-colour maps of Sicily and the outlying islands pinpoint sights you'll want to see.

In short, this handy guide will help you enjoy your trip to Sicily. From a peaceful fishing village to the thrill of peering into the smoking crater of Mount Etna, from the colourful markets to tantalizing *antipasti* and seafood, Berlitz tells you clearly and concisely what it's all about.

Let your travel agent help you choose a hotel. Let a restaurant guide help you find a good place to eat. But to decide "What should we do today?" travel with Berlitz

Area specialist: William Tuohy
Photography: Kurt Ammann
We're very grateful to the Italian State Tourist Office (E.N.I.T.) and the Provincial Tourist Boards of Sicily for their help in the preparation of this book. We also wish to thank Fabio Rapisardi for his valuable assistance

Contents

Maps: Palermo p.25, Palermo and Vicinity p.34, Sicily p.38–39, Syracuse p.53, Aeolian Islands p.75.
Photos: Cover, Santa Maria la Nuova in Monreale; pp. 2–3, Sicilian puppet theatre.

How to use this guide

If time is short, look for items to visit which are printed in bold type, e.g. **Castello Ursino.** Those sights most highly recommended are not only given in bold type but also carry our traveller symbol, e.g. **Mount Etna.**

The Island and its People

Sun-warmed Sicily, the largest island in the Mediterranean, is a haunting land of evocative, varied beauty—and dramatic extremes. It is a country of forbiddingly harsh mountains and beguilingly soft beaches, of isolated hilltop villages and colourful teeming cities, of humble fishing shacks and vast, opulent palaces. If its people are sometimes proud and aloof, they are more often warm and gregarious.

Though Sicily is part of Italy, most Italians think of it almost

as another country. And Sicilians often feel the same way about the rest of Italy. You'll find the post boxes in the main cities separated into two categories: "Sicily" and the "Continent".

Actually the history of Sicily goes back much further than that of the mainland. And as

Goethe wrote: "It's impossible to understand Italy without knowing Sicily, for Sicily is the key to it all."

This singular island has at-

Looking down on sandy lagoons of Tindari. In port, budding skipper works hard to keep vessel shipshape.

tracted visitors from the legendary Ulysses to English writer D.H. Lawrence. Tourists of every generation have been captivated by the mountains, forests, citrus groves, flowers, beaches and stunning secondary islands. And beyond the natural beauty, you'll find the inheritance of an immensely rich cultural past. Here are Grecian temples, Roman amphitheatres, Byzantine chapels, Arab baths, Norman cathedrals, Swabian castles and baroque churches in indigenous Sicilian style.

But the monuments are only part of the attraction. Sicily can also be a place to get away from it all. Many parts of the island are relatively free of crowds. In the interior, traditional Sicilian life goes on, unchanged by the 20th century. And along the sea there are miles of unspoiled beaches with clear water. What's more, in summer the sun shines an average of ten hours a day.

Standing at the crossroads of the Mediterranean—mid-way between Europe and North Africa, the Strait of Gibraltar and the Levant—Sicily has been a magnet since earliest times. First came the Greeks, who called the island Trinacria, meaning three-cornered. A profusion of others followed—

Romans, Byzantines, Arabs, Normans, Swabians, Angevins, Spaniards and Austrians—and shaped Sicily's history. You can see their architectural imprint in sites and structures all over the island.

When it comes to natural attractions, Sicily also has much to offer. Within its 9,926 square miles the visitor will find, among other things, Europe's largest volcano, the regal Mount Etna, hovering over citrus groves, vineyards and bougainvillea blossoms. You can walk to the bubbling crater, or ski the slopes in winter.

Sicily's shores provide a variety of beach and hill resorts. On the east, there's flower-bedecked Taormina, a favourite of the ancient Greeks. The riviera-like northern coast is lined with broad beaches, rocky coves, flowered villas and handsome cities set against steeply rising mountains. Palermo, whose cathedrals, palaces and gardens make it one of the unforgettable cities of the Mediterranean, caps that coast. The south-western shore, the least visited by tourists, is

Let the pungent aromas guide you round Sicily's tempting markets.

replete with beaches and fishing villages and crowned with the archaeological marvels of Agrigento and Selinunte.

Inland, you'll find another world: rough countryside with austere towns perched on the summits of hills and mountains. Here the farmer's donkey cart, women dressed in black and blood feuds still prevail. But this once inaccessible region has been opened up by a network of good roads, so that you can now reach almost any point on the island in a few hours by car.

You'll find Sicily's satellite islands among the most fascinating in the Mediterranean. Best are the Aeolians—volcanic Stromboli, with its smoking plume trailing in the sky, Vulcano and Lipari. Other outlying, more remote islands—like Ustica, the Egadi, Pantelleria and Lampedusa—are popular for archaeological research, underwater exploration and water sports.

This panorama of natural beauty is the home of 5 million Sicilians. Unfortunately for the island, its chief export in the past has been not citrus fruit but talented people; and the problem persists today. Some of the most celebrated Sicilians have included authors Luigi Pirandello, Giuseppe Tomasi di Lampedusa; Alessandro Scarlatti and Vincenzo Bellini of the music world; and the great Renaissance artist Antonello da Messina.

Less effusive than most southern Italians, Sicilians don't go in for the dramatic Neapolitan gesture. Their movements tend to be more restrained, reflecting the inbred caution of a race which has survived and absorbed successive invasions. Though they may be reserved, the island's inhabitants are warmly hospitable, particularly to visitors showing an interest in local things.

Educated Sicilians speak two languages: standard Italian and the local dialect. You needn't feel embarrassed if your phrases aren't always understood; Italians often have difficulty communicating with Sicilians, too. But a smattering of English is common enough in most of the places you'll be visiting.

Sicilian cuisine is robust and delicious: pasta with savoury sauces and an abundance of seafood. The local wines are plentiful, too, and reasonably priced. Meals tend to be long and sumptuous, and the siesta hour is strictly observed.

Sicily then is a land of infinite variety—of sites and sun, sand

Stromboli's volcano puts on a sparkling show, particularly at night.

and sea—and an unhurried sense of living. Some 2,500 years ago, the Greek philosopher Empedocles observed that the people of Agrigento ate as if they were going to die the next day, and built as if they were going to live forever. For the late-20th-century visitor, that is not a bad heritage: you'll eat as if there were no tomorrow and see things designed for eternity. **11**

A Brief History

The history of Sicily is long, complex, rich, varied, sometimes confused and always violent. Mainly it is one of occupation by successive foreign powers. The first concrete evidence comes from the Palaeolithic period—the incised drawings and vivid painting found in the caves of Addaura north of Monte Pellegrino and on the western island of Levanzo.

During the Neolithic period, agricultural peoples from the eastern Mediterranean began migrating westwards, and many settled in eastern Sicily and the Aeolian Islands. A tribe known as the Elymians, who traced their ancestry to Trojan refugees, arrived on the northwest coast and settled in beautiful sites like Segesta and Erice. They maintained links with the Mycenean traders in the Aegean Sea. Sicily itself takes its name from the mainland Italian tribe, the Sicels, who sailed across the strait about 1000 B.C. and put down roots

on the eastern shores of the island. They soon moved inland for protection against sea-borne marauders. At Pantalica, you can see one of their old necropolises cut into the hillside.

The Greek Period

The Greeks themselves—Chalcidians from Euboea—established their first colony in Sicily at Naxos on the strategic Strait of Messina about 735 B.C. A year later, according to Thucydides, the Corinthians founded the most important overseas Greek city at Syracuse. During the next two centuries, the Greeks colonized most of eastern and southern Sicily—coming from Megara to settle in Megara Hyblaea and from Rhodes and Crete to Gela.

Meanwhile, some Phoenicians had established trading outposts in western Sicily at Motya (Mozia) on San Pantaleo and later at Palermo. Their interests were ultimately bound to clash with the expansionist Greeks.

For the Greek city-states had in turn founded colonies of their own on the island—Selinus around 650 B.C. and Acragas (Agrigento) in 582 B.C. These new centres prospered, and the inhabitants built

Bustling fishing port of Sciacca is built on site of ancient baths.

13

graceful temples to the benevolent gods which we can see today. Together Sicily and the settlements in southern Italy became known as Magna Graecia—or Greater Greece.

In the 5th century B.C., the city of Syracuse dominated eastern Sicily. It challenged the Carthaginians (who had succeeded the Phoenicians) in the western part of the island, and under the Tyrant Gelon repulsed the Carthaginian onslaught in a crucial battle in 480 B.C. at Himera on the north coast. In 413, the Athenians—wary of the emerging Sicilian power—attacked Syracuse and were decisively defeated. Sicily had won its spurs as an independent force. This was its golden age.

Over the next two centuries a succession of powerful rulers—Dionysius I, Timoleon, Agathocles and Hieron II—assured Syracuse's predominance in the Mediterranean. Agathocles extended the city's power to North Africa and he took the title "King of Sicily". It was the last time in the island's history that Sicily was ruled by Sicilians.

The rise of the Romans inevitably led to conflict with the Carthaginians who still controlled part of western Sicily. During the First Punic War (264–241 B.C.), Hieron II of Syracuse allied himself with the Romans, who won and took over all of Sicily—except Syracuse.

Roman Conquest

Syracuse was not so fortunate in the Second Punic War (218–201 B.C.). Having thrown in its lot with Carthage, it was sacked by the victorious Romans in 212 B.C. In the general confusion, the Romans killed Archimedes, the great mathematician of Syracuse. As the Roman empire expanded, Sicily lost its strategic importance, shrinking to a provincial outpost—a granary supplying wheat, olives and wine to the far-flung Roman legions and to the Romans themselves.

The slow decline of Sicily was abetted by the practice of giving prominent citizens and victorious generals huge estates, known as *latifundia*. These were worked by slaves and owned by absentee landlords. Cruelly repressed, the slaves revolted in the so-called Slave Wars of 135-132 and 104 B.C.

The island was administered by corrupt and brutal officials. The most infamous, Verres, prompted Cicero to speak out on the dismal state of affairs on Sicily. However, under Augustus (27 B.C. to A.D. 14), conditions improved somewhat. Sicily even became something of a hunting resort area for wealthy Romans. The magnificent Roman villa near Piazza Armerina, built around A.D. 300, will give you some idea of how they lived (see p. 74). Also significant are the Roman modifications of Greek structures at Taormina, Catania and Syracuse.

Christianity arrived in Sicily in the 1st century. St. Peter and St. Paul reputedly stopped by the island en route to Rome. You can visit the catacombs in Syracuse, dating from the 3rd to the 6th century. During the early Christian era, unhappily, many pagan Greek and Roman temples were destroyed.

Like the rest of Italy, Sicily

Dazzling mosaics decorate hunting lodge at Casale—perhaps the retreat of Roman Emperor Maximian.

was overrun by the barbarians in the 5th century—Vandals from North Africa and Ostrogoths under the mighty King Theodoric. Then the Byzantines, led by General Belisarius, took the island in 535. In 663 Emperor Constans II transferred his court from Constantinople to Syracuse, but his stay was brief: he was assassinated in 668.

Sicily owes its reputation as a land of lemons largely to the Arabs.

Arab Rule

Next came the Saracen tide. The desert Arabs swept out of Arabia conquering all of the North African littoral, and the combined Arab-Berber forces landed on Sicily at Mazara del Vallo in 827. The Byzantines resisted bitterly. Palermo fell in 831, but Syracuse held out until 878. By then the Arabs had gained control of the whole island.

They made Palermo their capital, and the city flourished as one of the world's great centres of art, science and scholarship. The Arabs introduced citrus fruits, sugar cane, melons, cotton, date palms and pistachio nuts, and improved and extended the irrigation of the land. The Moslems were tolerant, allowing the Christians and Jews of Sicily to practise their religions.

The Names Remain

Though the Arabs may not have left much behind in the way of architecture, their imprint survives in other areas.

You will notice that many high sites in inland Sicily, settled by the Arabs for defense reasons, have the word *kalt* meaning fortress in their names. There's Caltanissetta (Fortress of the Virgins) and Caltagirone (Fortress of the Caves).

Mongibello was what the Arabs called Mount Etna. *Monte* and *djebel* (Arab for mountain) makes the "mountain of mountains". Names containing *ala* (Allah) are also common. Zappala means servant of God; Marsala, the harbour of God.

The Norman Invasion

Arab rule lasted from 827 until 1061. Then the Saracens, weakened by internal dynastic quarrels, fell to a small, resolute band of knights from Normandy under the leadership of Roger and Robert de Hauteville. These tough soldiers, the adventurous sons of Norman barons, had journeyed far and wide as able leaders in the Crusades. Having gained possession of southern Italy, they cast covetous eyes on the lovely land of Sicily.

In 1061 Roger took Messina, in 1072 Palermo, and by 1091 the Normans controlled the whole island. Roger (also known as Roger I) took the title of Count of Sicily and provided strong central administration, plus a willingness to absorb the previous Greek, Roman, Byzantine and Arab cultures. In 1130, his son, Roger II, was crowned King of Sicily and Naples. He initiated a burst of building, unprecedented since ancient Greek times. You can see these magnificent Norman churches and palaces—a mixture of Norman strength, Grecian grace and Arab fantasy—in Palermo, Monreale, Cefalù and Syracuse.

Roger II's reign was the zenith of Norman power in the Mediterranean. He was succeeded by his son, William I, known as "The Bad", a weak, pleasure-seeking king, and his grandson, William II, known as "The Good", a more enlightened ruler who unfortunately died early without a male successor. Next came Tancred, an illegitimate grandson of Roger II, elected by the Norman barons. But the new king was challenged by the Holy Roman Emperor Henry VI of Hohenstaufen. As the husband of Roger II's daughter Constance, he claimed the throne of Sicily. Henry eventually won out. When Tancred died, he deposed the infant son, William III.

So began the rule of the Swabian House of Hohenstaufen in Sicily. Henry was succeeded by his son Frederick, crowned Frederick I of Sicily and later Frederick II of Germany and the Holy Roman Empire. One of the giants of the Middle Ages and the true successor to Roger II, Frederick was known as *"stupor mundi"* (the wonder of the world). He was learned, fair-minded and efficient; he built castles, promoted culture and established a splendid court in Palermo.

Frederick was also a fine poet who encouraged early efforts in the Italian language. Deeply devoted to Sicily, he is reputed to have declared: "God would not have chosen Palestine for his own if he could have seen my Kingdom of Sicily."

His multiple roles—German King, Holy Roman Emperor and King of Sicily—brought Frederick into conflict with the Vatican. When he died in 1250, this power struggle continued. Frederick's bastard son Manfred succeeded him in Sicily, but the pope countered by appointing Charles of Anjou, brother of the French king. Charles defeated Manfred in battle, and the Angevins took over.

Charles earned the hatred of the Sicilians by launching a campaign of repression in his new realm. The tense situation culminated in the famous Sicilian Vespers of 1282. On Easter Tuesday, a French of-

18

Medieval castle of Erice incorporated remains of Venus' temple.

ficer insulted a Sicilian bride on her way to evening service in church. The populace reacted by massacring most of the French garrison on the island. In the War of the Vespers that followed, the Sicilians were aided in their rebellion by Peter of Aragon, a Spanish prince who had married Manfred's daughter. The Sicilians accepted him as king, along with the House of Aragon and four centuries of Spanish rule.

The Spanish Period

The Aragonese kings spent most of their time trying to dampen the conflict between the warring factions of Norman barons and Spanish nobles on the island. In 1410, the last member of the Sicilian branch of the Aragons died without a successor. The Spanish then proclaimed Ferdinand of Castile the legitimate monarch, and he reigned from Spain. Later, Sicily was governed by viceroys. With absentee rule, the introduction of the Inquisition and corrupt administration, Sicily sank into a political morass, and the Renaissance which revitalized northern and central Italy virtually passed it by. The island was further stricken by the eruption of Etna in 1669 and disastrous earthquakes in 1693 that destroyed many communities. Nonetheless, during the period the Spanish ruled the island, dozens of baroque churches and palaces were built giving Sicilian cities much of their visual aspect today.

After the wars of the Spanish succession, the Treaty of Utrecht (1713) ceded Sicily to the Piedmont House of Savoy. But seven years later, with the Treaty of the Hague, Sicily went to Austria. Austrian rule was so unpopular that when the Spanish prince Charles of Bourbon came to conquer the Kingdom of Naples in 1734, he was greeted with open arms. Charles, a progressive, moved on to become King of Spain. He was succeeded by his incompetent son, Ferdinand I, "King of the Two Sicilies" (Sicily plus southern Italy).

Ferdinand cared more for Neapolitan court life than administering the affairs of Sicily. When the French republicans under Napoleon marched against Naples, Ferdinand fled to Palermo aboard Admiral Nelson's flagship. For services rendered, Nelson was made Duke of Bronte by Ferdinand.

In 1815, after the defeat of Napoleon, Ferdinand and his successors continued their sorry rule of the island—favouring the nobles, repressing the poor and sabotaging any attempts at land reform of the huge absentee-owned *latifondi*.

Reunification and After

In 1848-49 Sicilians made an unsuccessful attempt to overthrow the corrupt Bourbons. Revolution was in the air. The Sicilian lawyer and patriot Francesco Crispi appealed to Giuseppe Garibaldi, the firebrand military leader of the Risorgimento movement which sought the unification of Italy. Garibaldi landed at Marsala in 1860 with his red-shirted "Thousand". They marched on Palermo and Messina, defeated the Bourbon troops and freed Sicily from foreign domination. Garibaldi then crossed the strait to drive the Bourbons from Naples.

The unification of Italy came in 1870. But the new régime, headed by the House of Savoy, was not altogether popular in Sicily. Northern rule meant that Sicily and southern Italy were consigned to the status of poor relations, forming a sort of backward colony of the rapidly industrializing north. By 1900, Sicily had become a major source of emigration, mainly to the United States.

During Sicily's period of Spanish rule, the organization known as the Mafia came into being. It grew out of the Sicilian custom of settling personal wrongs among themselves, since official justice was both foreign and incompetent. Surrounded by the code of silence, or *omertà*, the "honoured society" dispensed its own justice. While at first the Mafia may have served to protect the weak and to help fellow Sicilians, it evolved into a corrupt, repressive and criminal organization. Mussolini had some success in controlling the Mafia. But it remains an integral part of political and economic affairs today.

In 1943 the Allies chose Sicily as the first target for invasion. The British, under Field Marshal Montgomery, and the Americans, under General Patton, landed on the southern and eastern coasts of the island. The Sicilian campaign lasted only 38 days, but some cities bear the scars from the pre-invasion aerial bombardment. The Italian surrender was signed near Cassibile on the east coast.

In 1946, Sicily was granted a certain amount of regional autonomy from Rome, and the following year a Sicilian parliament was elected. Under continuing Sicilian pressure, the Italian government has begun allocating more funds to the island for its long-delayed development.

Where to Go

Sicily is so brimful of visual riches—cities, temples, churches, mountains, beaches—that there is no single "right" way to discover the island. Most bus tours start at one of the three principal ports of entry—Palermo, Messina or Catania—and circle the island, clockwise or counter-clockwise. These bus excursions provide a comfortable and convenient means of seeing major sights in a short time. Other visitors prefer rail travel; service between the larger towns is quite frequent.

However, if you have the time and money, the most practical way to see Sicily is by rented car. You can get to most points on the island in a few hours' time on good roads.

Many visitors begin their exploration of Sicily from the capital of Palermo. So let's start there.

Palermo
Pop. 650,000

Once an important Mediterranean centre, Palermo possesses the somewhat seedy grandeur of former greatness. Now the capital of Sicily, it is a large, spacious and colourful city set on the sea on the plain of Conca d'Oro (Golden Shell) between two magnificent headlands.

Palermo is raucous and lively, as befits one of Italy's main seaports. You'll find the backstreets hung with washing, broad boulevards for strolling, outdoor cafés for people-watching, and gardens filled with palm trees and cacti. The city air is redolent with spices and the aroma of Palermo's Oriental past, borne on the warm winds from North Africa.

Founded by the Phoenicians between the 9th and 6th centuries B.C., Palermo remained a Carthaginian stronghold until the Roman conquest in 254 B.C. In later days, it was occupied by the Saracens (831–1072), who made Palermo a brilliant centre of Arab civilization, rivalling Cairo in the East and Cordova in the West.

Modern and more traditional methods of agriculture coexist.

2.

The rule of the Normans in the 11th and 12th centuries was another high point—the golden age of art and architecture in Palermo: Byzantine, Arab and Norman elements were blended into a unique Sicilian-Norman style. The Normans were followed by the Hohenstaufens of Swabia, the Aragons and the Spanish Bourbons. Garibaldi liberated the city in 1860. During World War II, Palermo was badly damaged by Allied air attacks.

Among the famous Palermitans to be cited: the composer Alessandro Scarlatti and Giuseppe Tomasi di Lampedusa (1896–1957), whose book *The Leopard* is a brilliant portrayal of the Garibaldi period.

Starting right in the centre of the old city at **Quattro Canti** (Four Corners)—where Corso Vittorio Emanuele intersects Via Maqueda—you'll see a somewhat constricted sculptural assembly of baroque balconies, cornices, windows and niches. Fountains on each corner are topped by figures representing the four seasons, the Spanish kings of Sicily and finally Palermo's four patronesses (Saints Cristina, Ninfa, Oliva and Agata).

Next to Quattro Canti are the two main squares of the old city: **Piazza Pretoria** and **Piazza Bellini.** On Pretoria you'll find the Municipio (Town Hall), the church of Santa Caterina and a grandiose fountain with a score of nude figures done by Florentine sculptors in the 16th century. The fountain itself is circled by an iron fence, presumably to ward off vandals. And some Palermitans still call it "the fountain of shame" because of the naked statues, which supposedly shocked proper Sicilians when first unveiled.

You walk through an entry way into the adjacent Piazza Bellini, flanked by two of Palermo's most delightful churches. The tiny **San Cataldo** exemplifies the 12th-century Norman style, with its three miniature domes and Arabic inscriptions.

Cross a garden path to **La Martorana,** also known as Santa Maria dell'Ammiraglio (St. Mary of the Admiral) because it was begun in 1143 by George of Antioch, King Roger II's fleet commander. In the 15th century, it was presented to a convent originally founded by Eloisa Martorana, hence its popular name.

The church is studded with mosaics, some representing Roger II crowned by Christ; others depicting George of Antioch at the feet of the Vir-

gin. The mass, conducted according to the Greek rite with priests in sumptuous robes, is a strangely moving experience —the sound of lovely choral voices mixes with the smell of fragrant incense wafting through the church.

Along the Corso Vittorio Emanuele rises Palermo's massive **Cattedrale,** an imposing but erratic structure of golden limestone ordered in the late 12th century by William the Good's English archbishop. The original sturdy Norman building is overlaid with Gothic touches and crowned by an 18th-century baroque dome.

You'll find the interior airy but relatively austere. Buried in the cathedral's **royal tombs** are some of the greatest figures in Sicilian history: Roger II, his daughter, Constance, her husband, the Hohenstaufen Henry VI, their son, Frederick II, and his first wife, Constance of Aragon.

Even today, Sicilians come into the cathedral to pray at the tombs, and it is touching to see flowers placed before the crypt of Frederick II, more than 700 years after his death. But after all, he did make Palermo the cultural centre of Europe in the 13th century.

The **Palazzo dei Normanni** (Palace of the Normans) stands on the highest ground of the old city. An immense, imposing structure built on the site of an Arab fortress—like something

Santa Caterina church looks out
26 *over Palermo's "fountain of shame."*

out of a medieval romance—the *palazzo* has been reconstructed several times. It was the seat of government of the Norman kings and now houses the Sicilian parliament. Badly damaged by fire in 1944, the building's only original elements are the central section and the **Torre di Santa Ninfa,** also known as the Torre Pisana (Pisan Tower).

The palace's great artistic treasure, **Cappella Palatina** (Palatine Chapel), is hidden inside—upstairs and off the central courtyard. This chapel of the Norman kings, a perfect jewel, marvellously combines Byzantine-Arab and Norman

art. The wooden ceiling is a masterpiece of Moorish art with the carvings jutting down like stalactites. Dazzling gold and blue mosaics adorn the Byzantine cupola. With a towering Christ figure in mosaic over the altar and the Norman throne at the foot of the chapel, it seems almost as if the kings of heaven and earth met here to preside over Sicily.

Ask the custodian to open up the elegant **throne room** of Roger II inside the palace. There you'll find brilliant mosaics depicting hunting lions, gazelles, peacocks and swans fashioned by Arab artists under Persian influence.

And five minutes away is another prize of Arab-Norman architecture, **San Giovanni degli Eremiti** (St. John of the Hermits). Built in 1132 on the remains of a 6th-century Benedictine monastery, its picturesque pink domes and unusual shapes are widely reproduced on postcards as typical of the Moorish influence on Norman church design.

Adjoining the church (now deconsecrated) is a charming 13th-century cloister, overflowing with tropical plants and orange trees, a graceful blend of the Islamic and Christian styles.

Two of the most interesting museums in Italy are located in Palermo. The first, the **Museo Nazionale Archeologico,** contains priceless artefacts from Sicily's Grecian past. Housed in a 17th-century monastery, it has a section devoted to the major finds of the temple complex of Selinunte, with the celebrated **metopes** (panels in the frieze of a temple) taking top honours, as well as a vast collection of Grecian vases.

Among the other highlights: a magnificent Etruscan wine jug of black terracotta from central Italy; a 3rd-century B.C. bronze ram, by a Greek sculptor from Syracuse; and a Roman statue from Pompeii, *Hercules Slaying the Arcadian Stag.*

The second museum is near the port in the **Palazzo Abatellis.** This 15th-century building with a lovely interior courtyard has been turned into the National Gallery of Sicily. Superbly arranged, it contains some of the best examples of Sicilian medieval and Renaissance art. Chief among its treasures are a **majolica vase** of the 14th-century hispano-moresque style; a huge 15th-century fresco of unknown authorship, the dramatic *Triumph of Death;* Francesco Laurana's luminous sculpture, *Eleonora of Aragon;* a collection of works by Antonello da Messina, including his exquisite **Annunciation**—one of the finest paintings in all of Italy.

Tourists are sometimes advised to go to see some of Palermo's old residential palaces, like La Zisa and La Cuba. Unfortunately these buildings are either in a decrepit state, or inaccessible or under renovation, and visitors are often disappointed.

Palermo's gardens, on the other hand, are elegant and spacious. The Botanical Gar-

The local fishmonger's is as good a place as any to exchange views.

dens, the English Gardens, the Garibaldi Gardens are lush and fragrant, reminding you of the Orient and of Maupassant's phrase that Palermo "smells like a lady's bedroom".

For those with a taste for the macabre, there are the **Catacombe dei Cappuccini** (Via dei Cipressi). In the underground passages you'll find mummies galore—including the cream of Palermitan society.

Palermo's old port, known as **La Cala,** still plays host to a variety of fishing boats. A stroll along the quay can be interesting and colourful. Similarly, the **Kalsa,** the old Arab quarter of Palermo, is a casbah-like warren of alleys and vistas—run-down but lively.

The more fashionable areas of the city have shifted from the Quattro Canti to the spacious Viale della Libertà. On this broad boulevard and in the Piazza Castelnuovo, the Piazza Ruggero Settimo and the Piazza Verdi, Palermitans emerge after the blazing sun has sunk to stroll, chat with friends, sip the sweet aperitif liqueurs or enjoy melon ices or the *cassata gelata,* liquor-flavoured ice-cream with candied fruit.

Lush gardens and exotic red domes set off San Giovanni degli Eremiti.

Around Palermo

High up in the hills behind Palermo—with a superlative view of the Conca d'Oro and the sea—lies the bustling cathedral town of **Monreale.** Its name means the royal mountain of the Norman kings.

Here William the Good built a Benedictine abbey, which he graced with the most beautiful Norman church in Italy, **Santa Maria la Nuova** (1174-82). A kind of Palatine Chapel raised to enormous proportions, it's considered the highest expression of Italian medieval art. The interior is covered with glittering golden mosaics that tell the story of the Creation and other episodes from the Old and New Testaments, all dominated by a gigantic Christ over the apse. Included among the saints, oddly enough, is the figure of St. Thomas à Becket, painted only eight years after his death; William was the son-in-law of King Henry II of England. Round the chancel, chapels contain tombs of William, his father and other members of the family, as well as the heart of St. Louis of France. His body rested here in 1270 on the way home from Tunis.

Outside the cathedral, be sure to visit the fine **cloister.** The lush vegetation of the **31**

courtyard is surrounded by an arched arcade supported by 216 sets of twin columns, each with a different design and richly decorated capitals. In one corner you'll see an Arab fountain right out of the 1001 Nights. The cloister is closed on Thursdays.

The town itself is compact and pleasant, and from the various belvederes, or from the roof of the cathedral, the panorama is magnificent.

North-west of Palermo lies the great bulk of MONTE PEL-LEGRINO, which Goethe called "the most beautiful headland in the world". Near the top you'll find the **Santuario di**

Monreale: weird and wonderful carvings adorn cloister columns.

Santa Rosalia, dedicated to the patron saint of Palermo, a Norman princess who retired to a hermitage on the mountain.

The waters seeping from the mountain here are said to contain miraculous properties, and Palermitans flock to the site on July 11 to 15, and again on September 4, for colourful torchlight processions and fireworks. From the road you have a sweeping view of the harbour, the offshore islands, the mountains and, on a clear day, even Mount Etna.

On the other side of Monte Pellegrino, set in a tiny bay, is **Mondello.** With a mile and a half of velvety white beach and limpid blue waters, Mondello has been transformed from a small fishing village to one of the most popular seaside resorts in Sicily, offering tennis, riding and—for the hardy— winter bathing.

Farther to the west you come to the fishing community of SFERRACAVALLO and to a village and island both called ISOLA DELLE FEMMINE (Island of the Women), now popular for camping and bathing. Tourist villages are beginning to spring up all along this stretch of coast.

PUNTA RAISI is a newly developed resort complex near Palermo's airport. It's located on the eastern tip of the large crescent-shaped GOLFO DI CASTELLAMMARE, a place to find miles and miles of un-

crowded beach backed by mountains. You can pick your own spot here and be captivated by the violet colours of the sea.

Going east, the main road from Palermo runs through ROMAGNOLO, with beaches and several moderately priced fish restaurants, to BAGHERIA. Once the fashionable place for wealthy Palermitans to go, the town is known for its baroque summer villas, now sadly run down and for the most part closed to tourists. However, well worth a visit here is the museum dedicated to the works of the fine modern artist, Renato Guttuso, who was born in Bagheria.

The North Coast

Spectacularly perched above the sea on the slopes of Monte Catalfano, 18 kilometres east of Palermo, are the ruins of **Solunto.** Founded by Timoleon in the middle of the 4th century B.C., it was taken over and rebuilt by the Romans who gave it the name Soluntum or Solentum. Today, you can see the Roman plan, the foundations of buildings, houses, a theatre and water storage tanks and fragments of mosaics and wall paintings. Excavations are still continuing. The site is closed on Mondays, Wednesdays and Fridays.

The road east along the northern coast of Sicily runs through country reminiscent of the Ligurian Riviera: sandy beaches broken by rocky capes, fishing hamlets, flowering bougainvillea sprawled over walls, luxuriant vegetation, vineyards, myrtle and laurel trees and a mountainous backdrop.

TERMINI IMERESE is the site of a spa that has been famous since Roman times and the waters are said to be the ingredient that has made the macaroni from here famous throughout Sicily. Around the town you can find the usual traces of Roman civilization—bridges, aqueducts, amphitheatres and baths.

At IMERA lie the ruins of the 7th century B.C. Greek colony of Himera, destroyed by the Carthaginians in 409 B.C. Excavations are gradually bringing it to light. Look for the fragments of a Doric temple with four wide steps and column bases.

Cefalù, dating back to the 9th century B.C., is the pearl of Sicily's northern coast. Cicero described Cefalù—ancient Cephaloedium, which takes its name from the headland above—as "beautiful and prosperous". It remains so today, with its indigo and ochre houses and exceptional setting.

Cefalù's beaches are inviting, the old town charming and picturesque. In summer visiting yachts fill the fishing harbour.

But, above all, the city is known for its **Cattedrale,** one of the finest and best preserved examples of Norman church architecture in Italy. Begun by King Roger II in 1131, the graceful structure with its elegant golden façade and twin bell-towers dominates the old town. The baroque décor of the interior is gradually being stripped away to bare the austere Norman lines. But the cathedral's highlight remains untouched—the brilliant gold mosaics of late Byzantine design. Framed by Arabesque arches, the apse contains a powerful mosaic Christ clothed in blue. With glowing eyes and elongated features, this Christ looks strikingly modern.

Running parallel to the northern coast are the Madonie mountains with peaks up to 6000 feet, snow-covered in winter, and a cool refuge during hot Sicilian summers. You can visit one of the many charming villages set on the ridges.

Overlooking the Golfo di Patti on a promontory flanked by beach resorts is the town of TINDARI, known to the Greeks as Tyndaris. It was founded in 396 B.C. by Dionysius I of Syracuse and destroyed during the Saracen invasion. In the archaeological park, you'll find the remains of dwellings, shops, baths, the forum and a small gem of a Greek theatre, which the Romans used for gladiatorial contests. The small museum displays a model reconstruction of the ancient town.

Sicily's north-eastern coast has fine sandy beaches and seaside villages from which fishermen sally forth to harpoon swordfish.

Two highlights of northern coast— handcrafted ceramics and Cefalù.

The East Coast

Strategically located on the north-eastern tip of Sicily, **Messina** (pop. 260,000) is a modern port and the island's main gateway to continental Italy, with frequent car and passenger ferries. From the city and the hills above it, you'll have a splendid view of Calabria and the Aspromonte mountains across the Strait of Messina.

Messina was founded as Zancle by the Greeks in 730 B.C.—their key outpost in an area immortalized by Homer. It overlooked those twin threats of the ancient world, the whirl-

SICILY

pool of Charybdis and the rock of Scylla, the six-headed monster. Modern seafarers still have to watch out for the whirlpools arising at the juncture of the Ionian and Tyrrhenian seas. And the monster's rocky perch is present-day Scilla in Calabria. The fast-flowing waters of the strait churn up a harvest of deep-sea marine life—more than one hundred different species of fish have been identified here.

Messina, which had survived more than its shares of invasions and epidemics, was flattened by a disastrous earthquake in 1908. Nearly 100,000 people died in the catastrophe. The city was rebuilt with broad avenues and low buildings but again sustained heavy damage in the Allied air raids of 1943. Few old buildings remain.

The **Duomo,** ordered by the Norman King Roger II, was almost totally destroyed in the earthquake and again in the war. It has now been handsomely reconstructed and retains much of its original appearance—the sculpted façade, great Gothic doors and a dignified and spacious interior. There's a beautiful 16th-century fountain in the Piazza del Duomo.

The campanile houses what is said to be the world's largest **astronomical clock.** Each day at noon, a cannon announces its fantastic movements: the lion roars, the rooster crows, the angel hovers, the Madonna blesses, Christ appears, the dove flies, Death comes with a scythe, the days pass and the moon turns.

The **Museo Nazionale** (National Museum), to the north on the water's edge, is well worth a visit. You'll discover two powerful Caravaggios, *The Adoration of the Shepherds* and *The Resurrection of Lazarus* as well as works by Francesco Laurana and Antonello da Messina. Antonello (1430–79) is Messina's most famous son, a master of the Italian Renaissance.

A string of pleasant beaches stretches south along the Strait of Messina, crowned by the internationally famous resort of **Taormina.** This is a must on every visitor's list. From its perch 675 feet over the sea, you'll enjoy one of the most impressive views anywhere— the long sweep of coastline, rugged Calabria across the strait and the brooding bulk of Mount Etna to the west.

Messina's parade of the Giganti features town's legendary founders.

Taormina's streets are lined with outdoor cafés, small boutiques and benches in lively little piazzas. The light is soft, the ambiance warm, the view glorious. But be forewarned: the town, the approach roads and nearby beaches are jammed in midsummer. So unless you are prepared to spend a good deal of time in traffic, try to come here off-season when

Taormina has everything—a balmy climate, year-round bathing, superb views and one of the ancient world's finest theatres (next page).

you can enjoy Taormina at its best.

The town, founded in the 5th century B.C. by Dionysius I of Syracuse, was a vacation spot even in its earliest days. Its well-preserved **Greek theatre** dates from the 3rd century but was rebuilt by the Romans. Noted for its fine acoustics, it is

the second largest in Sicily. From the upper seats, you'll marvel at the view of the coast. They present classical plays here in June and August and films in July during the Taormina Film Festival.

The town's main street, Corso Umberto, affords you a pleasant stroll, and you should take a look at the austere **cathedral,** begun in the 13th century. It's one of the lovelier small churches in Sicily. The Palazzo Corvaia served as the seat of a Sicilian parliament in 1410.

German Field Marshal Kesselring used the fine old monastery and cloister of San Domenico as a headquarters in 1943. The gardens are superb. Now it's a luxury hotel, but you can go in for a drink.

Above Taormina you'll see the medieval castle on Monte Tauro, and even higher—for those who don't mind the altitude—the fortified village of CASTEL MOLA (1540 feet), which has the best view of all. Try the local almond wine.

During the summer season, a cable car runs every ten minutes or so from Taormina down to the beaches and restaurants along the shore.

The array of fragrances and the profusion of colours, along with the incomparable setting, **43**

give flower-filled Taormina a decidedly sensuous air. This quality has been prized by artists, many of whom live and work here.

Just south of Taormina, next to modern GIARDINI, the dedicated tourist will find NAXOS, where the first Greeks landed on Sicily in 735 B.C. Naxos was not well located and never amounted to much more than a small town, though travellers to Greece used to make sacrifices here. Recent excavations have uncovered traces of old wells, a small temple and the remains of houses.

From anywhere on the north-eastern coast of Sicily, you can't miss the dominating bulk of **Mount Etna.** It's the largest active volcano in Europe with a circumference around the base of some 125 miles. Because of the broad cone, the summit doesn't appear as high as it is—about 11,000 feet. Actually, the precise altitude varies, depending on the configuration of the summit after the most recent eruption.

Etna's flanks are covered with rich volcanic soil. The lower slopes bear a lush crop of citrus fruits—oranges, tangerines, lemons—as well as figs, almonds, grapes and olives. Higher up are forests of oak,

Mighty Etna

The Greeks imagined Etna as the forge of Vulcan, god of fire. It was also the home of Cyclopes, the one-eyed cannibal giants. The philosopher Empedocles was said to have leaped into the crater to his death to insure immortality.

The volcano has been credited with some 150 significant eruptions. Pindar noted a severe one in 475 B.C. At various times, lava has reached the coast. In 1669, Catania was partly engulfed by the hot flow.

During this century, volcanic activity has been increasing. The village of Mascali was wiped out in 1928. The most recent important eruption occurred in 1971 when lava destroyed the observatory of the Catania University Institute of Volcanology. Brooding, steaming Etna is capable of activity at any time.

pistachio, umbrella pine and eucalyptus trees. Near the summit, however, the terrain becomes barren, little besides ash and hardened lava.

The summit itself is pockmarked with small craters from which hot gases and lava sometimes burst forth. The area is patched with yellow sulphur stains.

You can reach the upper heights of Mount Etna by bus

or car from Catania or Taormina. The road ends at the RIFUGIO SAPIENZA at 6,260 feet, where you'll find a hostel, restaurant and the lower terminus of the cable car.

A ten-minute cable car ride speeds you up to the next stage at 8,200 feet. The upper tramway is undergoing repairs after the 1971 eruption, so you transfer to land rovers that go all the

Standing on the brink—visitors peer into crater of ever-active Etna.

way up to the summit. The last short stretch to the edge of the crater must be covered on foot. But the sight of bubbling lava in the crater, particularly at sunrise or sunset, is an unforgettable one.

You should check on the current arrangements for guides and transport to Etna's summit with travel agents in Catania or Taormina. The vehicles to the top run only from May to October, the rest of the year the summit is buried in snow, and ski lifts operate from the top of the tramway. Remember, too, that it is windy on Etna even in summer, so wear warm clothing and sturdy shoes for walking on the sharp terrain.

West of Etna is the town of BRONTE which gave its name to the duchy bestowed on Admiral Lord Nelson by the grateful King of Sicily, Ferdinand IV, in 1799 (see p. 20).

South-east of Etna, on the coast known as Riviera dei Ciclopi, you will find a series of pleasant, sandy bathing beaches topped by baroque towns—ACIREALE, ACI TREZZA and ACI CASTELLO. They take their names from Acis, the shepherd in Greek mythology slain by the Cyclops Polyphemus because of his love for Galatea. Acireale is the home of the Pennisi di Floristella numismatic collection. Its Sicilian, Greek and Imperial Roman coins are among the finest specimens in the world. The tourist office can arrange a visit.

Off Aci Trezza, note the FARAGLIONI or Reefs of Cyclops, strange-shaped rock formations at the harbour entrance, supposedly the rocks hurled by the one-eyed giant Polyphemus after Ulysses blinded him with a burning stake. In Aci Castello see the restored Norman fortifications built of black volcanic rock.

Sicily's second city and seaport, **Catania** (pop. 400,000), dominates the plain south of Etna. An ancient Greek town, Catania was partly covered by the lava flow from the Etna eruption of 1669. What was left was then levelled by a dreadful earthquake in 1693. The whole city has been rebuilt.

City life centres around the Via Etnea, the main street ending up at the Piazza del Duomo, a Sicilian baroque ensemble that captures the essence of Catanian architecture. The Duomo, founded in the 11th century by Roger I, has been reconstructed several times and

After the wash is done and hung out to dry, it serves as a sunshade.

now has a baroque façade. From the rear of the cathedral you can see the original apse of the volcanic rock. Inside are the ashes of the most important rulers of the House of Aragon and the tomb of Catanian composer Vincenzo Bellini (1801–35).

On the piazza you'll be amused by the charming **foun-tain** of an elephant moulded out of lava, carrying a granite Egyptian obelisk. The town hall also faces on this square. Off to the south, you'll find the bustling meat and fish markets.

Via Vittorio Emanuele II leads past **Via dei Crociferi,** an attractive street of baroque villas and churches, to the **Teatro Greco** (Greek Theatre), recon-

Knowing shopper looks over the day's slithery catch. Venerable lava elephant, Catania symbol, has long trumpeted city's attractions abroad.

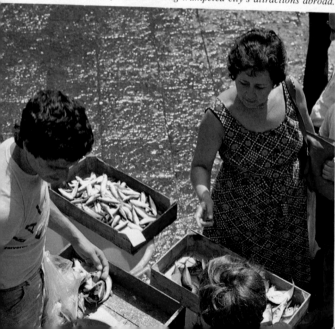

structed by the Romans, where orator Alcibiades sought to win Catanians to the cause of Athens in 415 B.C.

South of the theatre you'll find the **Castello Ursino,** built in the 13th century by Frederick II of Hohenstaufen and restored in 1837. It now serves as the Museo Civico (Municipal Museum). The interesting exhibits range from antiquity to the present day, with a sizable collection of Roman sculpture.

Catania is known for its gardens, especially those of the **Villa Bellini** in the centre of town, with a wide range of exotic plants and fragrances.

The road south of Catania, along the plain which bears its name, takes you past some bathing resorts with broad sandy beaches near pine groves.

The road also passes several new industrial zones on the way to Syracuse. The Sicilians are trying to concentrate these

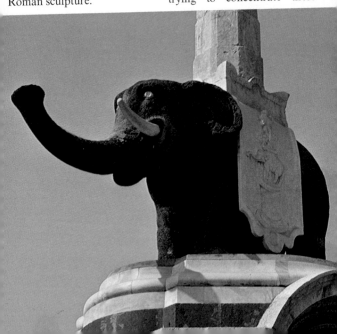

areas in a few places rather than scattering them all over the island.

At the end of a rough road near AUGUSTA, you can see the ruins of MEGARA HYBLAEA, founded by the Megarans of Greece toward the end of the 8th century B.C., and wiped out by the Romans in 214 B.C. There is also a small museum.

The city of **Siracusa** (Syracuse) was once the diadem in the crown of overseas Greek colonies, the rival of Athens for supremacy in the ancient world. Today a city of some 110,000, at its height Syracuse numbered more than 300,000, the largest community in Sicily.

The town was founded in 734 B.C. by Greeks from Corinth who drove out the native Sicels. The Greeks first settled on the island in Syracuse harbour, Ortygia, which they later connected to the mainland with a causeway. Today it's the Città Vecchia (old city).

In 413 B.C., Syracuse defeated Athens in a great battle, putting the Athenian admiral Demosthenes to death, and imprisoning the Athenians in the massive mainland quarries. So began Syracuse's great period of power.

Syracuse was governed by a succession of absolute rulers, known as tyrants. One of these,

Dionysius the Elder (406–367 B.C.) defeated the Carthaginians and made Syracuse master of Sicily and the western Mediterranean. Dionysius (or his son) was the one who feasted Damocles under a suspended sword.

The city was the home of the great mathematician and scientist Archimedes. When he discovered his principle of water displacement after a bath, he supposedly ran naked through the streets, shouting "Eureka!" (I have it!) The absent-minded Archimedes, absorbed in a problem, was killed by a Roman soldier, when the Romans took Syracuse in a siege that lasted from 214 to 212 B.C.

The Romans in turn were supplanted by the barbarians. The city went into decline, arrested only for the few years (A.D. 663–668) when the Byzantine Emperor Constans II made Syracuse his capital. The Arabs overran and destroyed the city in 878. Though freed from the Saracen yoke in the 11th century, Syracuse never again regained its former importance. In World War II, its port was the target first for Allied bombers and later for German aircraft.

Today, the archaeological zone lies on the mainland side of the city in the ancient quarter

SYRACUSE

of Neapolis on a site overlooking the Ionian Sea. The superb **Greek Theatre,** the most celebrated of Syracuse's ruins, is the best preserved outside Greece. With nine sections of 46 rows of seats hewn out of rock, it is also one of the largest (453 feet in diameter). You can see classical plays performed in June.

Close to the theatre is the **Latomia del Paradiso** (Paradise Quarry) where prisoners were held within the steep rocky walls. Now the quarry is overgrown with orange trees and oleanders. Inside, children delight in the **Orecchio di Dionisio** (Ear of Dionysius), so named by the painter Caravaggio—a huge cave shaped something like an ear lobe and noted for its unusual acoustical properties. Legend has it that the Tyrant Dionysius kept his prisoners in this cave so that he could listen to their conversations through a crack.

Here, too, you will find the beautifully shaped arena of the Roman **amphitheatre.** Note the entrance for gladiators and wild beasts.

Nearby is the **Catacombe di San Giovanni** (Catacombs of St. John) with the 4th-century crypt of martyred St. Marciano, said to be the first Christian church in Sicily. The wide-ranging St. Paul supposedly preached here.

The old island of **Ortygia** is delightful to wander through, with winding streets passing baroque palaces and off-white buildings hewn from the limestone quarry on the mainland. There are sudden, surprising views of the sea and the port—the best natural harbour in Sicily. And be sure to explore the **cathedral** in the Piazza del Duomo, one of the most fascinating in all Italy.

The first church here was built in the 7th century over and around the Greek temple of Athena, incorporating Corinthian columns in the exterior wall and the nave. The Normans rebuilt the church, and after the earthquake of 1693 it was adorned with a monumental late-baroque façade. Today, the cathedral represents an extraordinarily moving fusion of styles, pagan and Christian, dating back 2,500 years.

On the Piazza del Duomo, you'll also find the **Museo Archeologico Nazionale.** Though the arrangement is provisional during a transitional period before moving into new quarters in the Villa Landolina, this is an important museum with examples of native Sicilian pieces and a superlative collection of 5th- and 4th-century

B.C. **Greek vases,** sculptures and reliefs.

Among the other treasures are a statue of young *Hercules* (3rd century B.C.), Archaic sculptures from Megara Hyblaea and an excellent collection of original Sicilian coins. The museum is closed on Monday.

A famous spot in the old city is the Fonte Aretusa, a fountain

Splendid Greek vase from National Archaeological Museum collection.

surrounded by papyrus. According to the legend, the nymph Arethusa pursued by the river-god Alpheus threw herself into the sea and re-emerged as a spring on Ortygia. Though next to the sea, the fountain produces fresh water.

Another museum worth visiting is housed in the **Palazzo Bellomo,** a lovely 13th-century Swabian building. There are fine specimens of medieval art, an intense *Annunciation* by Antonello da Messina and an interesting collection of Sicilian furniture and armour.

At the tip of Ortygia Island, the huge **Castello Maniace** guards the promontory. Frederick II built the palace and fortress where Italian military forces are now quartered.

The Piazza Archimede in the centre of the old city is adorned by the Fountain of Artemis and several medieval palaces. On the Piazza Pancali, you'll find the **Tempio di Apollo,** probably the first temple in Sicily (7th–6th century B.C.). The rather fragmentary ruins have gone through a succession of stages —Greek temple, Byzantine church, Arab mosque, Norman

Early morning mass draws the faithful to Syracuse's cathedral.

basilica. It is best seen by illumination at night.

Along the canal that separates Ortygia from the Syracuse mainland are several fine restaurants where you can enjoy fresh fish, local white wine and an invigorating view of the harbour.

About 8 kilometres northwest of Syracuse, the **Castello Eurialo** (Castle of Euryalus) is the oldest Greek fortification. These massive stone works, the most elaborate of ancient times, were begun by Dionysius I to protect Syracuse on the landward side and later extended. It was here that Archimedes was said to have used a combination of mirrors and lenses to harness the sunlight and set the sails of the Roman fleet afire during the siege of 214–212 B.C. You can walk through the defence works—moats, internal corridors, cisterns, thick walls—a complex system of fortification indeed. Closed Mondays.

For those with a liking for prehistoric sites, the best in Grecian Sicily is located about 54 kilometres north-west of Syracuse: the necropolis at PANTALICA. Only a few stones remain of what is presumed to have been an old Sicel city, but some 5,000 tombs from the 13th to 8th century B.C. have 57 been hollowed out from the cliff walls. Be forewarned, though, the road leading to the site is a poor one.

The south-eastern corner of Sicily has become very popular with sea and sun enthusiasts who relish the wide, sandy and uncluttered beaches. You have a good choice of resorts, tourist villages and camping sites along this coast.

Pantalica's vast prehistoric necropolis honeycombs limestone cliffs.

The South-West Coast

The inland road from Syracuse to Gela takes you through the charming city of **Noto,** a fine example of Sicilian baroque with its broad vistas and gold-coloured buildings. It was almost entirely reconstructed after the 1693 earthquake. Outstanding are the cathedral and the Palazzi Ducezio and Villadorata. Then on to **Ragusa,** a picturesque city built on two levels. The old town below, on the site of the Sicel settlement of Hybla Heraia, is laced with beautiful baroque churches—see especially San Giorgio—and palaces.

A higher winding road from Syracuse to Ragusa passes through PALAZZOLO ACREIDE with its ruins of the ancient Syracusan colony of Akrai, founded in 664 B.C. What's left includes an attractive Greek theatre, an agora (market-place) and quarries. You'll also see tombs with Greek inscriptions and rock-cut dwellings from the Byzantine period.

Gela on the south-west coast was renowned for its pottery. Founded by Greeks from Rhodes and Crete in the 7th century B.C., it became one of the most important city-states in Sicily. The Greek dramatist Aeschylus died here in 456 B.C., supposedly after being hit by a tortoise shell dropped by a passing eagle.

But Gelon, the Tyrant of Gela, transferred the capital to Syracuse after 480, and Gela began to decline. It was destroyed by Carthaginians in 405, repopulated and then sacked once again around 280 B.C. It was only resurrected in the 13th century by Frederick II.

Passeggiata

As the summer sun sinks, Sicilians like to engage in the traditional pre-dinner stroll, the *passeggiata*, around the central piazza or main boulevard. This custom has its counterpart in other Mediterranean countries. Young men and women and their elders promenade for a couple of hours, specifically to see and be seen.

In a conservative society with strict rules against casual dating, this is the way for the young people to see one another and for their parents to evaluate marriage prospects.

New clothes will be shown off, confidences exchanged, and gossip passed along. For the tourist it is a pleasant way to watch the inner life of a Sicilian community surface before dinner.

The sandy beaches of Gela admired by tourists today also attracted military planners, and the American amphibious invasion of Sicily in 1943 took place here and at Licata. A monument north of the city marks where the fighting took place.

Not much remains of ancient Gela, except for the fine 4th-century B.C. **Greek fortifications** of Capo Soprano along the western beach. But the **museum** is well worth a close look. It displays the painted Greek vases for which Gela was famous.

The outstanding archaeological site on the south-west coast is the Valley of the Temples at **Agrigento.** Here you will find a dozen matchless, honey-coloured ruins along a ridge overlooking a wide sweep of the Mediterranean coastline, a tribute to the Greek genius for establishing their holy places in harmonious settings.

Agrigento was founded in 582 B.C. by the Gelans and was known as Akragas to the Greeks. The Romans called it Agrigentum, the Arabs, Girgent, and the Italians, first Girgenti and only recently Agrigento. The great Doric temples surrounded by acacia groves and walls were built in the 5th century below the acropolis, which is now the modern city.

At the height of power, Agrigento attracted poets from Greece—like Pindar—and was the home of the philosopher Empedocles (c. 490–430 B.C.) after whom the nearby port is named. Agrigento is also the birthplace of the modern playwright Luigi Pirandello (1867–1936).

Eventually conquered by the Carthaginians and then the Romans, Agrigento declined in influence and dwindled in size, its temples sacked and pillaged by successive invaders. Still, the ruins are remarkable, set along the Via Sacra, or Sacred Way, amid almond trees which blossom beautifully in the spring.

Start your walk at the elegant **Tempio di Giunone** (Temple of Juno) at the eastern end of the Via Sacra. Enough is left of this graceful structure to dazzle the visitor, particularly when seen from a distance with its columns outlined against the azure sky at sunrise or sunset.

Next in line is the magnificent **Tempio della Concordia**

Rooftop vista of Ragusa, a split-level city built astride two hills.

(Temple of Concord), the best preserved at Agrigento and one of the finest buildings in all of Magna Graecia. The name is taken from a Roman inscrip-

tion found on the site. Historians believe the temple is in such good condition because it was used as a Christian church in the 6th century.

The **Tempio di Ercole** (Temple of Hercules) is probably the oldest structure in the complex: eight of its columns have been re-erected but the

Many local harvesters of the sea continue to work from small boats.

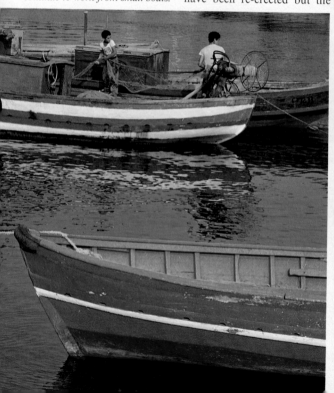

rest lie jumbled on the ground. Nearby, the **Tempio di Giove Olimpico** (Temple of Olympian Jupiter/Zeus) was one of the largest in the ancient world (173 by 361 feet), but alas, only a few of the original stones remain. Telemones, or columns, in the shape of human figures supported the entablature under the roof. One of these, Gigante (Giant), has been reassembled and can be seen in the Archaeological Museum.

The **Tempio dei Dioscuri** (Temple of the Heavenly Twins—Castor and Pollux) has only four columns left, but they are so exquisite that photographs of the ensemble often appear as a symbol of Agrigento. Actually, they are a 19th-century reconstruction. Across a stream lie the few remaining stones of what was the small Tempio di Vulcano (Temple of Vulcan). Stones and columns from the temples were used to fill the harbour at Porto Empedocle.

The **National Archaeological Museum**, adjoining the Church of San Nicola, is small but interesting: it combines the best in modern display techniques with a treasure trove of prehistoric and Grecian artefacts from Agrigento and Gela. You'll see amphorae, vases, craters, utensils, jewellery and larger fragments from the temples. The statue known as the **Ephebus of Agrigento** (5th century B.C.) is the prize piece in the collection.

The attractive 13th-century Church of San Nicola contains the **Sarcophagus of Phaedra,** a Roman work of the 2nd–3rd centuries A.D. with vivid scenes from mythology. The unusual holy water fount consists of a realistic hand holding a shell with the water.

Outside, you'll find the Comitium, a theatre-like assembly place dating from Greek times. Next to it the Oratorio di Falaride (Oratory of Phalaris) which is thought to be a 1st- or 2nd-century B.C. shrine that was converted to a Christian chapel in the Middle Ages.

Across the road from the museum, you can stroll through the excavated streets and foundations of the Roman city built around the Greek temple. The quarter was inhabited from the 2nd century B.C. to the 5th century A.D.

During the hot summer months, plan to visit the temples in the early morning or late afternoon—also the best times to take colour photographs. If you have a car, you can have a pleasant lunch at one of the several restaurants with terraces overlooking the Valley of the Temples, or, at the water's edge a couple of kilometres away at LIDO SAN LEONE, you can enjoy fresh seafood.

About 30 kilometres west of Agrigento is ERACLEA MINOA, established by the Selinutines and named after both Hercules and King Minos of Crete. The ancient city was ransacked and destroyed during the Punic Wars and there is not much left to see except for a small theatre and fragments of Greek fortifications.

SCIACCA, also started by the Selinutines in the 7th century B.C., is today a handsome city with a whitewashed, Moorish

Glossary of the Gods

Greek and Roman gods figure prominently in Sicily's cultural history, in particular the female, mother figure. The following are some of the island's most important gods, goddesses and assorted mythological figures, with the Greek and Roman equivalents:

Aphrodite (Venus), goddess of love and beauty. She had an important shrine at Erice and was often identified with indigenous Sicilian divinities.

Artemis (Diana), goddess of youth and the hunt, was the daughter of the supreme god Zeus, and the object of veneration by the Greeks in Sicily.

Athena (Minerva), goddess of wisdom, became one of the most popular divinities on the island, assimilating earlier cult figures.

Cyclopes, the one-eyed giants, were said to have lived in Enna and Etna. Blinded Polyphemus tossed stones at Ulysses from Sicily's eastern shore.

Demeter (Ceres), goddess of grain, who, grieving for her daughter Persephone, could cause famine and so was worshipped by Sicilian farmers.

Herakles (Hercules), Zeus' son, caught the imagination of Sicilians and his labours were depicted in Roman mosaics on the island.

Hephaestus (Vulcan), god of fire, was mightily feared in Sicily because of the volcanic activity of Mount Etna and the offshore islands.

Agrigento's Temple of Juno bears traces of a 5th-century B.C. fire. **65**

look, and imposing Renaissance churches and baroque palaces. But the heart of the city is the fishing port, one of the busiest on the island. You can watch the boats coming back to port, their sailors hustling trays of fish ashore—a rich harvest ranging from shrimps to squids and seabass. The seafood is auctioned off in a big dockside shed. Chanting the prices in Italian, the auctioneer quickly sells off each lot brought out for inspection.

Second only to Agrigento is the complex of temples at **Selinunte,** located on a gentle rise between what was once two harbours.

This settlement was founded by colonists from Megara Hyblaea in the mid-7th century B.C., the farthest the Greeks ever ventured into Carthaginian territory. It was named after the wild celery (Greek: *selinón*) you can still find growing in the fields.

The colossal temples were built in the 5th century, and the city was sacked by Hannibal during the wars with Carthage. But the complete devastation of the site, with no two stones left standing, was probably caused by an earthquake.

The ruins, in two major groups on either side of a dried-up river gorge, are designated by letters rather than names. In the eastern group, **Temple E,** a splendid Doric structure measuring 223 by 83 feet, has been reconstructed. Some of its beautifully carved metopes are now in the Palermo Archaeological Museum.

Temple F, north of it, was built earlier and is slightly smaller. It is in total ruins. Farthest north, **Temple G** is twice the size of the others, one of the biggest in Sicily. The drums that make up the columns weigh about a hundred tons apiece. Sadly, only a single column of Temple G remains upright in the aftermath of the quake.

West of the gorge, the other, smaller temples were built within the double walls of the **acropolis.** The north colonnade of **Temple C** has been reconstructed, the columns bearing part of the entablature (the frieze under the roof). The rest of the temples in the area lie scattered in pieces. What remains is an incomparable promenade by sunset with the stones glowing a golden colour.

At Selinunte, beware of hawkers who try to pass off figurines or coins as genuine articles from the site. Everything transportable of value has long since been removed.

The West Coast

After a stretch of sandy—and usually deserted—beaches, you'll reach the westernmost tip of Sicily, the ancient port of **Marsala.** It was founded by the Carthaginians (Lilybaeum) and was their chief link with North Africa. The name Marsala comes from the Arabs, who occupied the town and called it Marsal-Allah (Harbour of God). Garibaldi landed here with the Thousand on May 11, 1860, to wrest southern Italy from Bourbon domination.

For most people the name Marsala evokes the unique golden dessert wine. In 1773, Englishman John Woodhouse started shipping the local wine fortified with alcohol to Britain. Try to visit one of the exporting warehouses in Marsala, called *enoteca,* for a wine-tasting session. Every five years, some old wine is drained off and bottled, and new wine added. So when you sip a Marsala Stravecchio you may be sampling some drops of the same wine that Garibaldi's task force drank in celebration of their successful landing.

Just north of Marsala, on the islet of SAN PANTALEO, is the ancient Phoenician-Carthaginian community of **Motya** (now called Mozia). The town was sacked by Dionysius of Syracuse in 397 B.C. There are a few remains of houses, a necropolis and some fortifications. But the island is privately owned and you need permission (from the Amministrazione Whitaker in Palermo) to take the small boat across from the mainland.

The north-western coast of Sicily consists of a series of coves, rocky headlands and beaches, plus broad flatlands in geometric patterns. These are mostly devoted to salt pans dotted with windmills which pump up water to flood the fields. From here you have some striking views of the Egadi Islands (see p. 80).

The chief city is the thriving port of **Trapani,** from the Greek word *drépanon,* meaning scythe, because of the shape of the land jutting out into the sea. Trapani was a major base of the Carthaginians during their wars with the Romans. It also served as a main link with Spain during the rule of the House of Aragon because of its strategic location.

Today, Trapani is a fishing centre—the tunny season occurs in May and June—and the port for the Egadi Islands. You should visit, the 16th-century church of **Santa Maria del Gesù,** with its beautiful glazed **67** terracotta, *Madonna of the Angels*, by Andrea della Robbia. On the outskirts of Trapani, you'll find the **Santuario dell'Annunziata,** a graceful church with a Gothic façade. It contains another local treasure: Nino Pisano's highly venerated *Madonna of Trapani.* And, back in town, have a look in the old Jewish quarter, at the 16th-century **Palazzo della Giudecca** (Palace of the Jews) in ornate Spanish style.

About 14 kilometres east of Trapani—at a height of 2,461 feet—rises one of the most memorable sites in all of Sicily, ancient **Erice.** The Phoenicians and Greeks called it Eryx. And

with its lofty, unmatched position, you can understand why it became a holy place. Eryx on this rocky pinnacle was known to mariners throughout the Greek world for its temple to the goddess Aphrodite and the sacred courtesans who dwelt here.

Today, the town has an unspoiled medieval look—with Sicilian Norman houses on cobblestone streets, a charming 14th-century **Chiesa Matrice,** with a separate bell-tower built

Perched parapet of Castelletto Pepoli, Erice; Albanian traditions continue in Piana degli Albanesi.

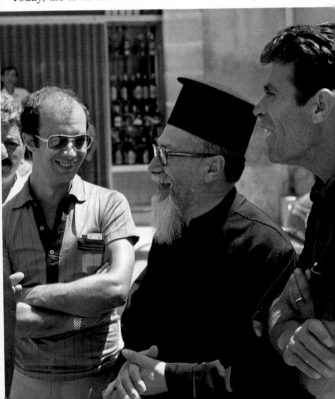

by Frederick II, all dominated by the castle which was begun in Norman times over an old Temple of Aphrodite. From this vantage point, you'll enjoy breathtaking **views** of inland Sicily to the east, the Egadi Islands to the west, and, in very clear weather, Pantelleria Island and Cape Bon in Tunisia to the south. You can reach Erice from Trapani by a road winding through the lovely pine groves, or by a cable car. A couple of hours in Erice is certainly worth the detour.

Between Erice and Palermo lies **Segesta,** one of the most enthralling sites in the Mediterranean. Standing alone and proud, the beautifully preserved but unfinished **Doric temple** of the 5th century. B.C. looks out across the pine-covered hillsides to the Gulf of Castellammare beyond. This once-thriving metropolis was badly damaged in wars between the Greek city-states and finished off by the Saracens in the 10th century.

Now, the temple stands in solitary grandeur. Set among the wild fennel, with goat bells tinkling in the distance, this elegant structure harmonizes perfectly with its surroundings. Further up on the mountain you come to the **theatre,** which has a superb view.

Inland Sicily

The interior of Sicily presents you with a vast spectrum of visual delights: a constantly changing landscape, dozens of dramatic hilltop towns, each with its Norman or baroque church, medieval castle and fortified walls. Among the most interesting:

Piana degli Albanesi is a small town populated by Eastern Orthodox refugees from Albania, who fled in the 15th century during the Turkish occupation of their land. Set high in the mountains about 25 kilometres south of Palermo, Piana degli Albanesi is known for its celebrations of the feast of the Epiphany and Easter when the townspeople don traditional costumes of baggy trousers and floppy shoes. Though the villagers nowadays are less inclined to celebrate festivals in costume, they still speak a dialect derived from Albanian.

Some 60 kilometres south of Palermo, you come across a town immortalized in modern fiction and film—CORLEONE,

Tiled stairs of Caltagirone ease the climb; typical inland scenes of sun-baked towns and furrowed fields (on the following page).

home of Don Vito Corleone of *The Godfather* fame. The city looks worn and forlorn standing above a barren plain on a rocky outcropping. People tend to think of Corleone as the ancestral home of the Sicilian Mafiosi, but it is an austere, withdrawn city that is not comfortable about its unwanted fame. The citizens, like most Sicilians from interior communities, are reserved and would just as soon not talk about *The Godfather*.

In ancient times the headquarters of the cult of Demeter (Ceres), **Enna** holds a commanding position in the geographical centre of Sicily at an altitude of 3,100 feet. Enna itself is capped by the impressive Castello di Lombardia, a medieval structure with 6 of the original 20 towers still standing. From the castle, you can observe all the major mountain ranges of Sicily as well as the great cone of Etna.

You'll see, too, Lago di Pergusa where Persephone, daughter of Demeter, was abducted by Hades to the underworld. She later became the goddess of vegetation in Sicily. Today's tourist can waterski on the lake.

Because of its height, Enna enjoys a reputation as a cool summer resort. This clean and orderly city has a 14th-century Gothic cathedral, rebuilt in a baroque style, and a tower erected by Frederick II. The public gardens are charming, and the view is immensely satisfying.

Between Enna and Gela, the hilltop city of PIAZZA ARMERINA has attracted widespread attention because of the nearby **Villa Imperiale** (at CASALE) with its dazzling Roman mosaics. This elaborate villa in a glen of silver birches and eucalyptus is thought to have been the hunting lodge of a wealthy titled Roman, perhaps Diocletian's co-emperor Maximian, whose patron was Hercules.

With its many rooms and sumptuous decorations, the villa rivals that of the Emperor Hadrian outside of Rome. Mosaics done during the 2nd and 3rd centuries A.D. adorn the floors of many rooms in the villa. In colourful and graceful design, they depict the labours of Hercules, hunting and fishing scenes, and wild animals from North Africa including elephants, lions and leopards.

Be sure to see the mosaic group that shows ten women gymnasts engaged in sports. Clad in two-piece bathing suits, they have come to be known as the "girls in bikinis".

The mosaics at Casale are considered to be the last great example of pagan art in Europe; thereafter, Christianity dominated artistic work.

More modern mosaics can be found at CALTAGIRONE, a great ceramics centre. Leading up to the Santa Maria del Monte is an impressive **flight of steps** decorated with blue-and-yellow majolica tiles. The local museum traces the development of Sicilian pottery.

Offshore Excursions

The Aeolian (or Lipari) Islands

A remarkable archipelago off the north-eastern coast of Sicily, the Aeolian Islands are named, according to the ancients, after Aeolus the God of the Winds, who is supposed to have kept the winds in a cave here. The islands attract tourists today because of their iso-

Sun sets over Aeolian isle of Vulcano, a place to unwind and dream.

lated, volcanic beauty—tortured shapes with lunar landscapes, remote coves and grottoes—and the underwater fishing and exploring. Seven are populated: Vulcano, Lipari, Salina, Filicudi, Alicudi, Panarea and Stromboli.

Vulcano, closest to Sicily, is a smoking mass of lava, though the last serious eruption was in 1890. Steam and gases still issue through the fumaroles, or vents, and you'll notice the strong smell of sulphur in the air. Some bathers like to take the sulphur baths in the hot pools here, caking themselves with mud. But you can also swim in the warm waters of the Baia di Levante, where the sea close to the beach is heated by underwater hot springs.

Lipari is the largest and most

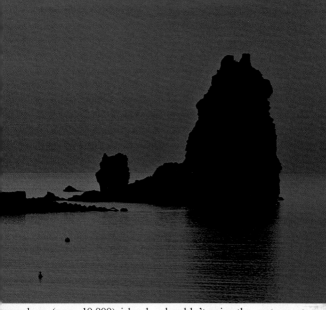

populous (pop. 10,000) island in the group. A motor tour of it will take you past the characteristic volcanic formations that have left large deposits of obsidian, a glassy black rock, and white pumice stone, the island's chief export. You can pick up your own samples from the side of the road.

Lipari town is still unspoiled, and the local castle contains a museum of indigenous culture dating back to prehistoric times. Even on a short visit, you

shouldn't miss the restaurants in Lipari. The fresh fish there are as tasty as any in the entire Mediterranean.

Stromboli's volcanic cone trails an ever-present plume of smoke seeping up from its simmering interior. The rich volcanic soil produces fine Malvasia grapes and a delicious dessert wine.

The island's volcano is active and you can walk up to the rim of the crater in about three hours' time for a close look. **77**

Easier on the legs is taking a boat trip and watching the lava run down a fissure called the Sciara del Fuoco (Pit of Fire). The spectacle is especially brilliant at night.

Stromboli has its own distinctive style of architecture: whitewashed Moorish-style houses with outside staircases built on narrow winding streets.

During the summer season, boats and hydrofoils operate daily between the Aeolian Islands, Milazzo, Messina, and even Palermo and Naples. Off season, there is daily service between Lipari and Milazzo. It is best to check with local travel agents for the current schedule.

Other Islands

Ustica, another volcanic island, stands alone 36 miles north-north-west of Palermo in the Tyrrhenian Sea. There you'll

On Stromboli, luxuriant vegetation frames whitewashed houses; donkey can negotiate the steep streets.

find remote beaches, grottoes and an abundance of underwater flora and fauna. The variety of marine life—grouper, mullet, lobster, bass, octopus, cuttlefish, scorpionfish—attracts scuba diving enthusiasts. An annual competition takes place in July. The fish and coral formations in the limpid waters are also popular with underwater photographers. In summer, there is daily boat service between Ustica and Palermo.

Favignana, Levanzo and Marettimo, together with a cluster of islets, form the **Egadis,** a tranquil archipelago off the north-western tip of Sicily. There are fine out-of-the-way beaches, amazingly clear water, fascinating grottoes with stalagmites, and good sports fishing, particularly tunny.

The whitewashed villages seem remote from Europe. On Levanzo, important examples of prehistoric art with fishing and hunting scenes have been found in caves. A daily boat service links the Egadi Islands with Trapani.

Lying in the Strait of Sicily, **Pantelleria** is closer to Tunisia than Sicily. A volcanic island whose summit reaches 2,743 feet, Pantelleria has had a long and violent history because of its strategic position on the trade routes of the Mediterranean. It was first colonized by Phoenicians and became an important Carthaginian base. It fell to the Romans in 217 B.C. and was later pillaged by the Barbary pirates. In World War II, as an Axis base, Pantelleria was pounded by Allied bombers. It surrendered on the eve of the invasion of Sicily in June 1943.

Pantelleria's attraction today is its remoteness, its prehistoric sites, the view from Montagna Grande of Europe and Africa, the hot baths and the beaches from which to go skin diving. The local wine is delicious and so are the lobsters with capers. In short, a marvellous place to escape to. There are boat services several times a week from Porto Empedocle and Trapani, and air flights from Trapani and Palermo.

The three barren **Pelagic Islands** are located some 200 kilometres south of Sicily between Malta and Tunisia. Lampedusa, with its high rocky cliffs, is noted for good fishing; Linosa of volcanic origin has served in the past as a sort of prisoners' island; and Lampione is uninhabited. There is a boat from Porto Empedocle and air service between Lampedusa and Trapani and Palermo.

What to Do

Folklore and Festivals

A strong strain of religious feeling mixed with a sense of medieval romance runs through Sicilian culture. The figure of the Madonna tends to dominate the religious festivals held at frequent intervals in Sicily. But the Norman knights are the heroes in the popular *opera dei pupi*, the puppet theatre.

Each town and village has a patron saint, and the members of the local community usually celebrate their holiday, or *festa*, on the saint's day. Depending on the religious circumstance, some *feste* are lively and light-hearted, others solemn and sombre. And in another reflection of Sicily's pagan past, there are festivals in the spring and summer, honouring various crops and fruits. Some of these are celebrated by the townspeople, in traditional dress, with elaborate processions.

The leading characters in the puppet theatre are modelled on the Norman conquerors—Roger, Tancred, Orlando—and the shows relate their battles with the Saracen defenders of the island. In this reflection of the golden age of chivalry

Ever present on festive occasions, the flautist with his friscalettu.

knights are either fighting the Arabs or jousting for the hands of fair maidens. In a well-staged *opera dei pupi* you'll see the gleam of armour, the flash of swords, limbs severed from **81** bodies, and even what appears to be blood on the victims.

The puppet theatres can be found in most major cities. They tend to be small, family-run enterprises located on back streets, for they have lost ground to mass entertainment in recent years. Be sure to double-check on the times and places before you start wandering around looking for the theatres.

Scenes from Norman con-

Stirring scenes from Sicily's history embellish horse and donkey carts.

quest also appear on the hand-painted sides of the donkey and horse carts (*carretti*) that used to be so common in Sicily. These panels show the knights battling with the Saracens, but they also move on through history, depicting the Sicilian Vespers, as well as the landing of Garibaldi and his Thousand in Marsala and their subsequent campaign.

On the cultural side, Palermo has a six-month opera season; Catania's is somewhat shorter. Trapani and Taormina hold music festivals. You can see classical plays given during the summer in the ruins at Syracuse, Segesta and Tindari.

Major Festivals

January 6. Epifania (Epiphany), a present-giving day, with a special Eastern Orthodox ceremony at Piana degli Albanesi, where some women wear Albanian costumes. The Palermo celebration is also splendid.

February 3-5. The Festival of Santa Agata, patron saint of Catania.

First week February. Almond Blossom Festival in Agrigento.

Easter. A Maundy Thursday procession at Marsala and Caltanissetta; a reenactment of the Stations of the Cross by penitents on Good Friday at Trapani; a passion play in Gela.

Corpus Christi. Processions, richly decorated with flowers, in Petralia Sottana (in the Madonie Mountains) and other towns.

May. Rally of brightly painted Sicilian carts and costumed dancers in Taormina.

May 10. Festival of Saints Alfio, Filadelfo and Cirino with a pilgrimage to the sanctuary at Trecastagni on the slopes of Mount Etna.

June 3. Festival of the Madonna della Lettera, protectress of the city of Messina.

July 11-15. Festival of Santa Rosalia, Palermo's patron saint.

Mid-August. Palio dei Normanni, parade in medieval costume at Piazza Armerina, commemorating arrival of King Roger and his knights.

August 15. Ferragosto, the Assumption of the Virgin, the biggest summer holiday in Italy, with festivities in many towns.

September 4. Santa Rosalia procession up Monte Pellegrino at Palermo.

September 8. Pilgrimage of the Madonna at Tindari.

November 1-2. All Saints' Day, followed by the Day of the Dead, when cemeteries are visited and masses sung in honour of the dead.

December 31. Vigilia di Capodanno. New Year's Eve, with services in the larger churches, often accompanied by fireworks.

Shopping

Though not in the same league for shoppers as Rome, Florence or Venice, Sicily does have good buys in handicrafts and local specialities.

Among the more eye-catching items is pottery—ranging from fine and highly decorated enamelled plates, which they have been making in the area around Collesano since the 16th century, to rougher, more primitive models. The ceramics tend to be colourful, serviceable and reasonably priced. You might also be interested in the lovely terracotta figurines dressed in 18th-century costumes.

Sicily is noted for the fine embroidery done by women on the island. The work resembles old brocade. The shawls are exquisite and the lacework, fine. In some of the northern mountain communities, they still weave carpets by hand using vari-coloured pieces of cloth in Byzantine and Arab patterns. You can find bargains in these woven rugs and tapestry-like skirts in Taormina. Or try the vividly coloured saddle-bags which make handsome over-the-shoulder carry-alls.

Another island speciality is metalwork. Interesting candelabra worked from iron or other metals can brighten up any room. Or you might consider a knight in a suit of armour, originally produced for

Good buys: brightly painted pottery and fruit made of marzipan.

the *opera dei pupi*, now something of a collector's item.

Similarly, the old wood-paintings and panel carvings from the sides of Sicilian horse carts *(carretti)* have become popular, approaching antique status. If you can find them, you're in luck.

In north-eastern Sicily and the Aeolian Islands, look for the locally made jewellery. It is fashioned from the native coral, which grows offshore, and from obsidian, the black volcanic glass formed in previous eruptions. Local craftsmen make lovely bracelets, necklaces and brooches out of the material—and the prices are appreciably lower than on the mainland.

Palermo has a good flea market, filled with second-hand goods of every kind. For the knowledgeable, it's a marvellous place to browse around.

You might want to take some of Sicily's sweets home to your friends or children. Particularly recommended is marzipan, the famous almond confection shaped and coloured like natural fruits. And as a liquid souvenir, a bottle of Marsala.

As for bargaining, in Sicily this traditional practice often takes the form of a "discount", called *sconto*. You might suggest that the seller offer you a *sconto*, perhaps rounding off the price to the next lower figure: e.g. an 11,000 lire article evened off at 10,000.

Remember that most shops shut for several hours at siesta time but they remain open until the early evening.

A word of warning: don't expect to find the real thing if you are offered antiquities by hawkers at an archaeological site. All the genuine articles have long since been unearthed. On the other hand, if you find the reproductions attractive, by all means, purchase one—not as an authentic artefact, but as a tourist's souvenir, priced accordingly.

Sports

Swimming

The island of Sicily is ringed with bathing beaches of every description. They range from wide velvety strands to pebbly coves. You can find luxurious resorts with umbrellas, mattresses and beach boys, as well as deserted stretches of sand, where you can be far from the crowds.

The littlest bather can enjoy the calm waters and sunny skies.

The most developed beaches are on Sicily's northern and eastern coasts near Palermo, Cefalù, Messina, Taormina and Catania. These often have umbrella pines or acacias as a background, and you can either go to a free beach or to a club with an entrance fee. Less developed and more primitive are those places along the south-western coast where you can

A dunking is part of the fun for even the best-balanced windsurfer.

pull your car up behind a beach and have it all to yourself. Most of Sicily's best archaeological sites are near the sea, and after a hot day of sightseeing, a dip in the Mediterranean is the best way to cool off.

Sicilians once took their beaches for granted, and only city dwellers used them much.

But with the coming of northern tourists—attracted by long hours of sunshine in the summer months—an increasing number of beach resorts and tourist villages are springing up.

Generally speaking, Sicilian beaches are safe. There is little tide and few places have a strong undertow. But you might inquire whether there is a lifeguard available.

The usual bathing season is from March to November except for hardy Nordics who find the Mediterranean swimmable all year round.

Snorkelling and Scuba

Both snorkelling and scuba-diving have become popular along the Sicilian coast, especially around the off-shore islands, where there are coral reefs and plenty of undersea life. No permit needed.

The coast of Sicily is dotted with rocky outcroppings and grottoes that attract underwater enthusiasts. And the Aeolian, Egadi and Pelagic islands have become well-known as skin-diving centres. Best periods for subaquatic activity: March–May and September–October. Ustica Island holds a competition in underwater photography and fishing in July.

89

Boating and Water-Skiing

Many of the bigger resorts have small sailing boats for hire. You can also rent or charter larger vessels to cruise along the coast, but you should make arrangements for such extended trips beforehand.

Water-skiing has become popular in Sicily, not only at the seaside resorts but on the inland lakes. Several places have clubs, and you'll have no trouble finding water-skiing facilities at any of the major coastal resorts.

Fishing for lunch by historic Naxos.

Fishing

Sicilians are great fishermen, but mostly of the commercial variety. Nonetheless, you can arrange to charter a boat for deep-sea fishing. During the late spring and early summer, tunny congregate off western Sicily, and swordfish between the island and mainland Italy. For fresh-water fishing, a local permit is needed.

And, of course, the ordinary angler can always drop his line off a dock or cast a rod into the surf—and hope for the best.

Other Sports

Tennis is not a widespread sport on the island, but you'll find a few courts in large cities and resorts like Taormina. And these resorts, too, will usually have **riding** facilities.

Hunting is popular, mostly for hare, duck and fowl. A permit is required.

Sicily's mountains provide good ground for **hiking** in summer (contact the local Club Alpino Italiano or the tourist office for information) and for **skiing** in winter. You'll have to admit that skiing on a live volcano is a singular experience: all around the snowy slopes of Etna and above the gaping crater partially covered by clouds of sulphurous smoke.

Wining and Dining

From the most humble *trattoria* to the finest resort restaurant, Sicilian cooks take pride in making sure that you *mangia bene*, eat well. In Sicily you can eat both well and heartily— some would say heavily. The sauces are often piquant and olive oil is not spared in cooking. But in the best Sicilian cuisine, the accent is on freshness. For the island is a cornucopia of fresh fruits and vegetables, and the surrounding sea is an endless provider of a splendid variety of fish and shellfish.*

As befits an imaginative people, Sicilians have taken traditional Italian cuisine and added their own touch of fantasy, often with the flavourful overtones from the Greek and Arab past. Take, for instance, the conventional dish of spaghetti or macaroni. The Sicilians cook it *al dente*, which means slightly chewy, and then add fresh sardines, anchovies, pimento, raisins and saffron, creating *pasta con sarde*, a sophisticated speciality. Or to the common dish of broad beans, *fave*, they might add wild fen-

* For a comprehensive glossary of Italian wining and dining, ask your bookshop for the Berlitz EUROPEAN MENU READER.

nel *(finocchio)*—which grows everywhere—artichokes and basil, and then season it all with olive oil and lemon or vinegar, and *ecco!* you have a simple yet memorable dish.

Sicilian meals can be a major production: three or four courses spread out over a couple of hours. Most restaurants offer, in succession, an *antipasto* (hors d'œuvres) before the pasta, a pasta or soup course, the main dish of fish or meat plus a salad or vegetables, then cheese, fruit and a dessert. The meal is invariably accompanied by wine and mineral water.

All this may be a tall order, particularly on a hot summer's day when you don't feel hungry. But you can vary your order according to your stomach's mood and choose only a couple of courses. Don't be afraid to reverse the order. You might want to take only a pasta course and a salad or simply a main course with vegetables.

If you do as the Sicilians do, you'll order mineral water with your meals. The local water is quite drinkable, but drinking bottled water has become a custom. Either fizzy or still, it helps you to digest the sometimes heavy meals or dilute the effects of the wine on the stomach—or head.

Antipasto and Pasta

The larger the restaurant, the wider the assortment of *antipasti* on display. This invariably consists of cold dishes, often spiced or marinated: fish, salami, ham, olives, beans, aubergines, stuffed peppers, anchovies. You should try the mixed seafood, usually a combination of squid, shrimps, octopus in a lively blend of herbs, lemon and oil. Another favourite is *caponata*, a mixture of aubergine (eggplant), tomatoes, olives, capers and celery.

For your pasta course, you could choose *pasta con sarde*, or *pasta con broccoli, pasta e melanzane* (aubergine), or *pasta con aragosta* (spiny lobster), the very spicy *spaghetti al peperoncino* (with red peppers and garlic), *pasta al sugo di seppie* (squid ink), or a Syracusan speciality, *pasta con la Norma* (layers of macaroni, hard-boiled eggs, aubergines, *ricotta* and tomato sauce).

Main Dishes

If you're a devotee of seafood, you might wish to concentrate on the fish rather than meat. Almost every restaurant will offer fish as a main course. The north-eastern shores are the home of the swordfish (*pescespada*) in late spring and early summer, and a swordfish steak grilled with a sprinkling of lemon, capers and herbs is a dish fit for a Greek god. So too are the spiny lobsters caught around the Aeolian Islands. Prawns and shrimps abound in the seas off Sicily. They may be called *scampi, gamberetti, gamberoni* depending on the size and variety, and you can have them grilled, boiled or fried with bread crumbs. Try, too, the *sciabachedda*, tiny succulent fried fish, and tunny fish with onions (*tonno con cipollata*). Of Arabic origin, *cuscus di pesce*, made of semolina and chopped-up fish, is a favourite dish here. Then there's *fritto misto*, a deep-fried mixture of squid and shrimps. And soup with fish (*zuppa di pesce*) or with mussels (*zuppa di cozze*).

Meat—not one of the region's best products—tends to be more conventional in Sicily. Steak can be tough, pork is probably the best bet. But you should order *involtini alla siciliana*, slices of meat, usually veal, rolled around a filling of ham, salami, cheese, breadcrumbs and onion cooked over charcoal. Another Sicilian speciality is *falso magro*, a meat roll filled with sausage, ham, hard-boiled eggs and onions, cooked in tomato sauce. In season, try *capretto*, roast kid, **93** and when you see it, the rabbit *(coniglio)* prepared in a sweet-and-sour sauce.

It is always wise to ask the restaurant proprietor what his speciality is and what he recommends that day, rather than insisting on a specific dish you may have in mind.

Vegetables and Fruit

The island has marvellous fresh vegetables. You can eat them as a side dish, as a first or a second course, depending on your mood. This list is endless: tomatoes, artichokes, broccoli and *broccoletti* (tender young variety), spinach, carrots, beans, lentils, peas, peppers, fennel, celery, asparagus, onions, a wide variety of mushrooms and wild greens for cooking and exotic salads. Eat them fresh, cooked, marinated, fried or au gratin.

The fruits of Sicily are justly famed: mouth-watering oranges *(arancia)*, lemons *(limone)*, tangerines *(mandarino)*, grapefruit *(pompelmo)*, figs *(fichi)* and grapes *(uva)*. There are also melons *(melone)*, exotic prickly pears *(fichi d'India)* and a Japanese fruit called *nespole* here, not to mention nuts—almonds, peanuts and pistachio. Sicilians, by the way, eat orange slices with salt and oil. It's surprisingly tangy.

Cheese and Sweets

You can get a variety of Italian cheeses in Sicily, but don't pass up the excellent local products. From ewe's milk, there's *pecorino* or *canestrato* (called *tuma* when fresh, but often aged with black pepper), fresh *ricotta*, sweet or salted. *Caciocavallo* (sometimes smoked) and *provola* are gourd-shaped cheeses that come tied in pairs. *Mozzarella*, too, is popular. Mixed with tomatoes and basil and sprinkled with oil and pepper, it makes a fine first course.

Perhaps because of their Oriental heritage, Sicilians have a decidedly sweet tooth. You'll find a profusion of desserts on the island—cakes of every description and flavour, some laced with liquor-luscious ice-cream, puff pastry filled with *ricotta (cannoli)*, macaroons and almond biscuits. The best-known dessert of all is the *cassata alla siciliana*, a sponge cake with candied fruits, a dish the Sicilians picked up from the Arabs.

The ice-cream *(gelato)* is rich and fresh. Try the *torrone* (with nougat) or the *cassata gelata*, natural fruit sherbets of tan-

Gourmets laud Sicily's peerless fresh fish, vegetables and fruit.

gerine, lemon or melon, or a refreshing *granita*, crushed-ice flavoured with lemon or coffee.

Famed too are the local marzipan—candy of almond paste in natural colours shaped like fruits—candied fruits and *cubaita*, a crunchy mixture of honey, sugar and sesame seeds.

Wine

Sicilian wines are just beginning to be known outside the island—mainly because the best ones did not leave the island. Only poorer grades were exported, and they were used to bolster the alcoholic content of thin Italian wine.

Hearty and inexpensive, Sicilian wines are the best value on the island, and every restaurant will have a *vino della casa* (house wine) at a moderate price. But you can, of course, also order wines from the rest of Italy. The Sicilians aren't fussy about matching wines with dishes, so you certainly don't need to worry about which colour to order.

Corvo, produced on the northern coast near Casteldaccia, is the best-known local wine. The reds are strong and trustworthy, the whites smooth and dry. There is also a sparkling white wine—a lot cheaper than champagne for festive occasions.

The slopes of Mount Etna are the source of a number of delicious red *(rosso)*, white *(bianco)* and rosé *(rosato)* wines. *Etna Bianco* has a lively golden colour and a taste reminiscent of volcanic soil. The deep ruby-hued *Etna Rosso* improves with age; *Fuoco dell'Etna* is a lively red. Other wines produced around Etna include *Mascalucia, Nicolosi, Trecastagni, Viagrande, Zafferana, Randazzo, Castiglione, Linguaglossa* and *Misterbianco.*

A fine red wine called *Faro* comes from the north-eastern tip of Sicily. And in the highlands inland they make the excellent reds, whites and rosés of *Regaleali.*

The western regions produce *Bianco d'Alcamo*, a good, dry white wine with a slight, light-green colour to it. *Pignatello*, from the south-west coastal area. is noted for its rich crimson glow.

The best way to obtain a good wine is to ask the restaurateur to recommend a local one. When a Sicilian's pride is involved in a recommendation, you'll rarely go wrong.

Sicilians claim their wine soothes the troubled mind and induces a siesta-time of quiet contemplation.

The island's dessert wines are properly acclaimed, notably *Marsala*, *Zibibbo* from the southern coast, *Moscato* from Pantelleria and *Malvasia* from the island of Lipari. These fortified amber wines are a fine way to end your meal, accompanied by the strong black Sicilian coffee.

Besides dessert wines, there are many other local digestives—and aperitifs—which tend to be on the sweet side.

Restaurants, Bars and Cafés
In Sicily, restaurants are normally open from 12.30 to 3 p.m. and from 7.30 to about 11 p.m. Those in busy resort areas

end to close later, those in smaller towns, earlier.

Warning: all restaurants must now issue a formal receipt indicating the sales tax or VAT *(I.V.A.)*. A customer may be stopped outside the premises and fined if unable to produce a receipt. The bill usually includes cover *(co-perto)* and service *(servizio)* charges as well. It's customary to leave about 10% for the waiter.

Bars and snack bars stay open from early morning till late at night. Some serve sandwiches and instant pizzas and usually have cakes of various sorts. These establishments are popular among Sicilians for morning coffee and rolls *(cornetti)* and are handy for a quick snack or light lunch. You pay the cashier first and hand the receipt to the counterman when you order. You generally leave the small change as a tip.

Sicilian coffee is as strong as the usual Italian espresso. But you can dilute it by asking for *caffè lungo*—or for a *cappuccino* or *caffè latte*, which are served with hot milk. If you want it even stronger, ask for a *ristretto*. Coffee is always cheaper taken at the bar standing up than at a table.

Sicilians spend a lot of time in bars or outdoor cafés, sipping drinks, eating ices, reading papers and talking about politics or sports or the local gossip. Sitting in cafés is a pleasant way to pass the time and watch Sicilian life go by.

To Help You Order...

I'd like a table.	**Vorrei un tavolo.**	
Do you have a set menu?	**Avete un menù a prezzo fisso?**	
I'd like a/an/some...	**Vorrei...**	
ashtray	**un portacenere**	
beer	**una birra**	
bread	**del pane**	
butter	**del burro**	
coffee	**un caffè**	
cream	**della panna**	
dessert	**un dessert**	
fish	**del pesce**	
fork	**una forchetta**	

fruit	**della frutta**
glass	**un bicchiere**
ice-cream	**un gelato**
knife	**un coltello**
meat	**della carne**
milk	**del latte**
mineral water	**dell'acqua minerale**
napkin	**un tovagliolo**

olive oil	**dell'olio d'oliva**	soup	**una minestra**
pepper	**del pepe**	spoon	**un cucchiaio**
potatoes	**delle patate**	sugar	**dello zucchero**
salad	**dell'insalata**	tea	**un tè**
salt	**del sale**	wine	**del vino**

... and Read the Menu

aglio	garlic	**lamponi**	raspberries
agnello	lamb	**limone**	lemon
albicocche	apricots	**mela**	apple
al forno	baked	**melanzane**	aubergine (egg-
anguilla	eel		plant)
anguria	watermelon	**maiale**	pork
anitra	duck	**merluzzo**	cod
antipasto	hors d'œuvres	**peperoni**	peppers,
arancia	orange		pimentos
arrosto	roast	**pesca**	peach
braciola	chop	**pesce**	fish
branzino	sea bass	**polenta**	purée of maize
calamari	squid		(cornmeal)
carciofi	artichokes	**pollo**	chicken
cipolle	onions	**pomodoro**	tomato
coniglio	rabbit	**prosciutto**	ham
cozze	mussels	**(e melone)**	(with melon)
crostacei	shellfish	**risotto**	rice dish
dentice	dentex (a	**salsa**	sauce
	white fish)	**sarde**	sardines
fagiolini	green beans	**seppia**	cuttlefish
fegato	liver	**sogliola**	sole
fichi	figs	**spigola**	sea bass
finocchio	fennel	**spinaci**	spinach
formaggio	cheese	**tonno**	tunny fish
fragole	strawberries	**triglia**	red mullet
frittata	omelette	**trippe**	tripe
fritto	fried	**uova**	eggs
frutti di mare	seafood	**verdura**	raw
funghi	mushrooms	**cruda**	vegetables
gamberi	scampi	**vitello**	veal
gnocchi	dumplings	**vongole**	clams
insalata verde	green salad	**zuppa**	soup

100

How to Get There

The following information on types of fares, conditions and reductions is general and subject to change, so a reliable travel agent is indispensable for a well-planned holiday in Sicily whether you go by car, train, coach or plane.

From the United Kingdom

BY AIR: Daily flights leave from London for Palermo via Milan and Rome. There are six-day to one-month excursion fares. Students, young people, common interest groups and school groups are eligible for special reductions. You can also travel on an APEX fare (bought at least one month before departure) to Naples and connect with a flight or ferry to Palermo. In fact, there are direct flights from all major Italian cities to Sicily. Certain airlines offer a car for your holiday if two or more adult passengers travel on a tourist-class scheduled flight and stay at least seven days.

Charter Flights and Package Tours: There is a wide range of package tours available including a walking holiday with accommodation provided, an archaeological tour accompanied by a guest lecturer and other special-interest tours. Be sure to read the terms of your contract and consider cancellation insurance.

BY CAR: Best route perhaps is via Calais and Paris, Mâcon, Geneva through the Mt. Blanc Tunnel (Chamonix to Courmayeur) to Milan, Florence, Rome and Naples. Another, more scenic road goes by way of Calais, Reims, Basle, through the Gotthard Pass to Milan, then down the coast via Genoa to Naples. Your car is carried on a train through the Gotthard Pass.

It is possible for you and your car to travel by motorail from Boulogne or Paris to Milan and then on to Rome (all year round) or to Villa San Giovanni (summer only).

BY RAIL: The most economical route is via Rome, with an overnight connection to Sicily, a total of about 36 hours from London. You may break your journey anywhere en route. Direct trains will take you to Taormina, Catania, Enna, Syracuse or Palermo. Sleeping accommodation is available on international trains. See TRAINS in the Blueprint.

BY COACH: Europabus travels between London and Rome all year round. There are also buses from Rome to Naples daily (April to October).

From North America

BY AIR: Sicily's two airports, at Palermo and Catania, are linked with a dozen major cities in the United States and Canada. Non-stop service between Palermo and New York operate several times a week. Daily flights from Chicago, New York, Los Angeles, Utica, Seattle, San Francisco and Washington, D.C., go via Rome to Palermo, and from New York, San Francisco, Washington, D.C., and Toronto to Catania.

To date, there are no youth fares available to cities in Italy; APEX and excursion fares are the best buy in reduced fares. Conditions change constantly but in general APEX (Advance Purchase Excursion) tickets must be paid for several weeks in advance and cancellation penalties are stiff. The excursion fare, valid for a longer period, requires no advance booking and arrangements may be made for stopovers.

Charter Flights and Package Tours have been put together by several tour operators to Rome and the island of Sicily. One 15-day GIT (Group Inclusive Tour) features only Sicilian attractions. Also available are ITCs (Inclusive Tour Charters) to Rome that offer a cruise to Sicily and 5- to 8-day tours throughout the year.

When to Go

In Sicily, summer lasts almost all year, but the climate is generally mild at all times; it is only on the southern plains, near Africa, that the sea breezes do not compensate for the torrid sun. During the in-between seasons and in high altitudes, make sure you have some warm clothing.

The following chart gives an idea of the monthly average temperatures in Palermo:

	J	F	M	A	M	J	J	A	S	O	N	D
Air °F	59	61	63	68	76	83	87	87	83	76	68	6.
°C	15	16	17	20	24	28	30	30	28	24	20	1

	J	F	M	A	M	J	J	A	S	O	N	D
Water °F	57	57	57	59	63	70	76	79	76	72	67	6.
°C	14	14	14	15	17	21	24	26	24	22	19	1

Planning Your Budget

To give you an idea of what to expect, here are some average prices in Italian lire. However, remember that all prices must be regarded as approximate, as inflation creeps relentlessly up.

Airports. Porters L. 700 per bag. Bus to Palermo L. 1,600. Taxi Punta Raisi–Palermo L. 25,000–30,000, Fontanarossa–Catania L. 15,000.

Buses. Catania–Palermo L. 7,000 one way, Catania–Taormina L. 3,000.

Camping. L. 2,500–3,000 per person, L. 2,000–2,500 per tent.

Car hire. *Fiat 127* L. 18,300 per day plus L. 300 per km., L. 298,000 per week (unlimited mileage). *Fiat 131* L. 30,000 per day plus L. 360 per km., L. 438,000 per week (unlimited mileage).

Entertainment. Cinema L. 3,000–3,500, discotheque L. 5,000–6,000 (entry and first drink).

Ferries and boats (per person). Naples–Palermo L. 33,000, plus car L. 48,000. Villa S. Giovanni–Messina L. 8,500. Reggio–Catania L. 30,000–36,000 (with car). Messina–Aeolian Is. L. 3,600–10,000.

Hairdressers. Haircut L. 7,000, shampoo and set L. 7,000.

Hotels and accommodation (double room with bath per night). *Luxury* L. 70,000–90,000, *1st cl.* L. 40,000–50,000, *2nd cl.* L. 30,000–40,000, *3rd cl.* L. 25,000–35,000, *4th cl.* 11,000–20,000. *Youth Hostel* L. 3,000–500.

Laundry (ironed). Shirt L. 2,500, set of underclothes L. 1,000. *Dry cleaning:* sports jacket L. 2,500, trousers L. 2,500, dress L. 3,000, skirt L. 2,000, blouse L. 2,000.

Meals and drinks. Continental breakfast L. 2,000–3,000, lunch L. 10,000–15,000, dinner L. 10,000–15,000, coffee L. 350, beer L. 1,000, soft drink L. 1,500.

Moped hire. L. 3,500 per hour, L. 15,000 per day, L. 90,000 per week, L. 15,000 deposit.

Sightseeing. Museum and archaeological sites L. 750. Horsedrawn cabs L. 10,000 (Catania historical centre).

Taxis. Catania to Etna L. 40,000–50,000. See also prices under "Airports".

Trains (2nd cl. return). Rome–Palermo L. 47,200, Taormina–Syracuse L. 6,600, Catania–Mt. Etna (Ferrovia Circumetnea) L. 10,000 (minimum) to L. 30,000 (with visit of crater and refreshments), Catania (airport) to Taormina L. 1,800 (one-way).

BLUEPRINT for a Perfect Trip

An A-Z Summary of Practical Information and Facts

Listed after many entries is an equivalent Italian translation, usually in the singular. A star (★) after an entry title indicates that prices concerning this section can be found on page 103.

All facts were carefully checked before going to press, but changes are bound to occur, and we are pleased to hear about any new developments.

Contents

AIRPORTS* *(aeroporto).* Sicily is served by two major airports for international and domestic flights: Punta Raisi, 39 kilometres from Palermo (tel. 091-23 13 30) and Fontanarossa (tel. 095-34 63 38), 8 kilometres from Catania. Though charters sometimes fly directly to Sicily, you must change in Rome or Milan on scheduled non-Italian airlines.

Porters are available at both airports (no luggage trolleys). Both have snack bars serving sandwiches and drinks, as well as souvenir shops, news-stands and currency exchange offices *(cambio).* Neither has a duty-free shop or a restaurant.

Check-in time is 35 minutes before departure. A few hours before flight time, however, have your hotel receptionist telephone the airport to find out about any last-minute flight or transport delays.

Ground transport: From Punta Raisi it takes about 60 minutes by bus to get to the terminal in Palermo, located at:

Via Mazzini, 59; tel. (091) 58 45 33 (Alitalia office).

Catch the bus in front of the airport. Buses to the airport leave around an hour and a half before international flights.

From Fontanarossa the half-hour trip by city bus (number 24) starts from the bus-stop at the airport entrance for the terminal at the Piazza G. Verga in Catania. Buses leave almost every 30 minutes.

Taxis are available at both airports; be sure you agree on an approximate price in advance (see TAXIS).

Domestic flights: Frequent services link Milan and Rome with Sicily. There are local airports at Trapani, and on Lampedusa and Pantelleria; they all have bus services into town.

Porter!	**Facchino!**
Taxi!	**Taxi!**
Where's the bus for…?	**Dov'è l'autobus per…?**
What time does it leave/arrive?	**A che ora parte/arriva?**

BABYSITTERS *(bambinaia).* Although larger hotels and holiday villages can arrange for someone reliable to babysit in the summer season you won't find any specific organization offering this kind of service. You should try the local or provincial tourist offices or your hotel receptionist for possible leads. Note, however, that children are included in many activities in Italy (eating out, for example) which may mean staying up much later than customs back home allow.

Can you get me a babysitter for tonight?	**Può trovarmi una bambinaia per questa sera?**

B **BUSES*.** Inter-city services are recommended as the best means of public transport between towns and outlying areas since trains, although they do go everywhere, may be slow and more expensive. Many motorways cross Sicily giving you the chance to take in splendid views from the coach window. The trip from Palermo to Catania, for example, takes 2½ hours by coach, 5 hours by train! The principal company, S.A.I.S., has offices in most towns.

Palermo: For Trapani, Segesta, Selinunte, Marsala and Mazara del Vallo several different companies have buses which leave from Piazza Marina near the old harbour. For Messina, Taormina, Catania and Enna go to the S.A.I.S. office:
Via P. Balsamo, 16.

Catania: S.A.I.S., Piazza Teatro Massimo.

Taormina: S.A.I.S., Piazza San Pancrazio.

When's the next bus to…?	**Quando parte il prossimo autobus per…?**
Where's the nearest stop?	**Dov'è la fermata più vicina?**
Does this bus go to…?	**Questo autobus va a…?**

C **CAMPING*** *(campeggio).* Sicily has many camping possibilities. The major sites are listed in the yellow pages under "Campeggi e Villaggi Turistici". Most are equipped at least with electricity, water and toilet facilities.

You may camp freely outside of sites if you obtain permission either from the owner of the property or from the local authorities *(Municipio).* For your personal safety you should choose sites where there are other campers.

You may also contact the Ente Provinciale per il Turismo in major towns for comprehensive lists of camping sites, rates and facilities (which can vary widely). The Touring Club Italiano and the Automobile Club d'Italia publish lists of sites and tourist villages, which can be bought in bookstores or referred to in E.P.T. offices. If you'd like to write for information before leaving home send your request to Centro Internazionale Prenotazioni Campeggio, Casella Postale 649, 50100 Florence, Italy.

When you enter Italy with a caravan (trailer) you must be able to show an inventory (with two copies) of the material and equipment in the caravan: dishes, linen, etc.

If you'd like to hire a camper for at least five days, check at the E.P.T. offices in Palermo or Catania for conditions.

May we camp here?	**Possiamo campeggiare qui?**
Is there a camp-site near here?	**C'è un campeggio qui vicino?**
We have a tent/caravan (trailer).	**Abbiamo la tenda/la roulotte.**

CAR HIRE* *(autonoleggio)*. The major international car rental firms have offices in the main cities and at the airports; they are listed in the yellow pages. The hotel receptionist may be able to recommend an inexpensive local firm. You need a valid driving licence. Minimum age varies from 21 to 25 according to the company. A deposit is often required except for credit card holders; insurance is included. Most agencies offer a range of Fiats; larger Italian and foreign models are less frequently available. It is possible to rent in one Sicilian city and turn the car in at another.

I'd like to rent a car tomorrow.	**Vorrei noleggiare un'automobile per domani.**
for one day	**per un giorno**
for a week	**per una settimana**

CIGARETTES, CIGARS, TOBACCO *(sigarette, sigari, tabacco)*. These are sold under state monopoly in tobacconists' bearing a large *T* outside, or at hotel and café counters. Foreign brands cost as much as 50 per cent more than local products; cheaper Italian cigarettes are considered a bit rough by most foreign smokers, however.

Although tobacco products can be bought for less on the black market, the quality of the tobacco is not always good. Besides, pickpockets abound in the areas where contraband cigarettes are for sale, so these places should be avoided (especially at night).

| a packet of cigarettes/matches | **un pacchetto di sigarette/ fiammiferi** |
| with/without filter | **con/senza filtro** |

CLOTHING *(abbigliamento)*. From May to October in Sicily you should take along summer-weight clothes with a jacket or shawl for the evening. Rainwear may not be necessary during the dry Sicilian summer, but be prepared for showers in the late spring and autumn. If you're planning an excursion on Mount Etna, you should have warm clothes and walking shoes.

Though Sicilians are normally conservative in dress, they have become accustomed to the informality of tourists. Few restaurants insist

107

on ties or jackets for men. Some churches forbid too-short skirts, bare-backed dresses or other attire considered disrespectful, but it's no longer essential for a woman to cover her head. Bikinis are accepted on all Sicilian beaches but topless bathing is still taboo.

When buying shoes or clothing, the following conversion table should be useful (remember though that sizes vary somewhat according to manufacturers):

Women								
Clothing			Shirts / Pullovers			Shoes		
GB	USA	Italy	GB	USA	Italy	GB	USA	Italy
10	8	40	32	10	38	3	4½	35
12	10	42	34	12	40	4	5½	36
14	12	44	36	14	42	5	6½	37
16	14	46	38	16	44	6	7½	38
18	16	48	40	18	46	7	8½	39

Men								
Clothing			Shirts			Shoes		
GB / USA		Italy	GB / USA		Italy	GB	USA	Italy
36		46	14		36	6	6½	40
38		48	14½		37	7	7½	41
40		50	15		38	8	8½	42
42		52	15½		39	9	9½	43
44		54	16		40	10	10½	44

COMMUNICATIONS

Post Office *(ufficio postale)*: The main post offices in larger Sicilian cities are generally open every day (except Sundays) without a lunch break. You can send telexes, telegrams and express letters, and make overseas telephone calls. Stamps are sold in the post office or at a tobacconist's. Have your hotel clerk take care of stamping and mailing your letters if possible. Remember mail is slow, so send anything important *espresso* (express; special delivery).

Mail *(posta)*: Mail is unlikely to reach you in Italy, particularly if you're here for only a short time. For longer stays (if you don't know your address beforehand) you can have your mail sent in care of *fermo posta* (poste restante; general delivery) at the local post office. Don't forget to bring your passport for identification when picking up mail; a small fee is charged.

Telegram *(telegramma)*: Night letters or night-rate telegrams (minimum 22 words) are considerably cheaper than normal cables.

Telephone *(telefono)*: Public telephones are located in post offices and various bars and cafés indicated by a yellow telephone sign outside. Public phones require tokens *(gettoni)*, which you can purchase from the cashier at 50 lire apiece. After you insert the token, dial the number. Older boxes have a lever button which you must push when you get an answer. If you're calling an out-of-town number, you insert several tokens depending on the distance, and dial the area code or prefix *(prefisso)* before the number.

Phone books have all the local emergency numbers listed at the front: police, fire, medical assistance, long distance calls, automobile breakdowns, etc. The last page of the phone book gives translations of Italian headings.

To get the operator for Europe, dial 15; for North American or intercontinental calls, 170. To reverse charges you ask for *chiamata "r"*, pronounced "ay-ray".

air mail/registered	**via aerea/raccomandata**
A stamp for this letter/postcard, please.	**Per favore, un francobollo per questa lettera/cartolina.**
I want to send a telegram to…	**Desidero mandare un telegramma a…**
Have you received any mail for…?	**C'è posta per…?**

COMPLAINTS *(reclamo)*. In hotels, restaurants or shops, complaints should be made to the manager *(direttore)* or to the proprietor *(proprietario)*. If satisfaction is not quickly forthcoming, mention your intention to report the incident to the local tourist association, or, in case of more serious matters, to the police; in Palermo there is a special branch of the tourist police to handle serious complaints. The threat of a formal declaration to the police *(denuncia)* should be effective in matters like overcharging for car repairs. But if you get into any real trouble, such as a major car accident, call your embassy or consulate.

C   **CONSULATES and EMBASSIES** *(consolato; ambasciata).* All th
embassies are located in Rome but some countries maintain consu
lates in Sicily.

Canada: Embassy (Rome): Via G. Balieta De Rossi, 27; tel. (06) 85 53 4
Eire: Embassy (Rome): Via del Circo Massimo, 9; tel. (06) 57 82 43/4
United Kingdom: British Consulate General (Naples), Via Francesc
Crispi 122; tel. (081) 20 92 27
Embassy (Rome): Via XX Settembre, 80/a; tel. (06) 475 54 41
U.S.A.: Via Vaccarini, 1, Palermo; tel. (090) 25 30 16
Embassy (Rome): Via Vittorio Veneto, 119, tel. (06) 46 74

Where's the British/American consulate?	**Dov'è il consolato britannico/ americano?**
It's very urgent.	**È molto urgente.**

CONVERTER CHARTS. For fluid, tire pressure and distance mea
sures, see page 113. Italy uses the metric system.

Temperature

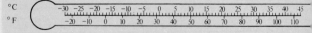

Length

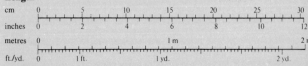

Weight

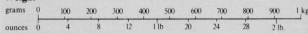

CUSTOMS FORMALITIES *(dogana).* Italian customs officials are
unlikely to quibble over smaller points; they are interested mainly in
detecting smuggled art treasures, currency or narcotics. If you're exporting archaeological relics, works of art, or gems, you should obtain
a bill of sale and a permit from the government (this is normally

110 handled by the dealer).

Each visitor (including children) may import or export 200,000 lire
in Italian currency. In foreign currency you may import unlimited
amounts, but to take the equivalent of more than 200,000 lire back out
of Italy you must present the V2 declaration form (filled out upon entry)
at the border.

Following is a chart describing what you may take into Italy duty-
free, and then which goods may be brought into your own country when
returning home:

Entering Italy from:	Cigarettes		Cigars		(grams) Tobacco	Spirits		Wine
EEC	300	or	75	or	400	1½ l.	or	3 l.
Europe non-EEC	200	or	50	or	250	¾ l.	or	2 l.
Outside Europe	400	or	100	or	500	¾ l.	or	2 l.
Into:								
Canada	200	and	50	and	900 g.	1.1 l.	or	1.1 l.
U.K.	200	or	50	or	250 g.	1 l.	and	2 l.
U.S.A.	200	and	100	and	*	1 l.	or	1 l.

* a reasonable quantity

I've nothing to declare.   **Non ho nulla da dichiarare.**
It's for personal use.   **È per mio uso personale.**

DRIVING IN SICILY. To bring your car into Sicily, you will need: **D**

International Driving Licence or a valid national driving licence
accompanied by a translation (free of charge from the Italian State
Tourist Office)
car registration papers
International Green Card or other insurance valid for foreign countries
national identity sticker for your car and a red warning triangle in
case of breakdown

D **Driving conditions:** Drive on the right, pass on the left. Traffic on major roads has the right-of-way over traffic entering from side roads, but this—like all other traffic regulations—is frequently ignored, so watch out. At equal intersections the car to the right has the right-of-way.

Sicilian drivers are impulsive and have quick reflexes. They expect others to drive the same way, so stay alert in traffic, particularly in the cities and be prepared for anything. Better slow down at key crossroads to follow signs and don't hesitate to ask directions. See also POLICE. Once off the main highways in Sicily you are likely to encounter farm animals on the road; so be on your guard, especially at night.

The new expressways *(autostrada)* are designed for fast and safe driving; secondary roads are good, too. Speed limits in Italy are based on the car engine size. The following chart gives the engine size in cubic centimetres and the speed limits (in kilometres per hour):

Engine size	less than 600 cc.	600 to 900 cc.	900 to 1300 cc. (and motorcycles more than 150 cc.)	more than 1300 cc.
Main roads	80 kph.	90 kph.	100 kph.	110 kph.
Motorways (Expressways)	90 kph.	110 kph.	130 kph.	140 kph.

Town speed limits are posted on the entry roads in kilometres per hour.

Breakdowns: Most service stations have a mechanic or someone who can make minor repairs, and garages are plentiful in Italy. Any can take care of a Fiat and foreign makes have agencies in the major cities. If you're in trouble out in the country, there's often a local mechanic who can improvise a repair to keep you going. You can dial 116 for emergency service from the Automobile Club d'Italia. Call boxes are located at regular intervals on the *autostrade* in case of breakdowns or other emergencies.

Foreigners with an international mutual assistance card issued by an affiliated automobile association are eligible for free breakdown service *(Soccorso Stradale Gratuito A.C.I.)*, including immediate repairs or towage. There are minimum call fees and of course you **112** must pay for any parts required.

Fuel and Oil: Fuel is available in *normale, super* and diesel. Oil comes in at least three types. Many service stations close between 12 and 3 p.m. In town, stations close around 7 p.m.

After abolishing petrol coupons, the Italian authorities are now trying to reintroduce them. When available, they can be bought outside the country at Italian National Tourist Offices (E.N.I.T.), at automobile clubs and some banks in country of departure, and at the Italian Automobile Club (A.C.I.) offices at the border (in foreign currency only). There are also some rebates on toll motorways—check with the tourist office.

Distance

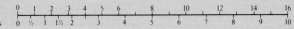

Fluid measures

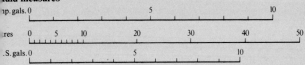

Tire pressure

lb./sq.in.	kg/cm²	lb./sq.in.	kg/cm²
10	0.7	26	1.8
12	0.8	27	1.9
15	1.1	28	2.0
18	1.3	30	2.1
20	1.4	33	2.3
21	1.5	36	2.5
23	1.6	38	2.7
24	1.7	40	2.8

Parking: There is generally no problem finding parking places but for safety's sake you are advised to park in a lot with an attendant or in your hotel's security zone.

Road signs: Most road signs in Sicily use the international standard code. But there are written signs too.

D

Accendere le luci	Use headlights
Curva pericolosa	Dangerous bend (curve)
Deviazione	Diversion (detour)
Discesa pericolosa	Steep hill (with gradient percentage)
Divieto di sorpasso	No overtaking (passing)
Lavori in corso	Road works
Parcheggio autorizzato	Parking allowed
Passaggio a livello	Level (railway) crossing
Passaggio limitato in altezza	Height restriction
Passaggio vietato ai pedoni	No pedestrians
Pericolo	Danger
Rallentare	Slow down
Senso vietato/unico	No entry/One-way street
Vietato l'ingresso	No entry
Zona pedonale	Pedestrian zone

(International) Driving Licence	**Patente (Internazionale)**
Car registration papers	**Libretto di circolazione**
Green Card	**Carta Verde**
Are we on the right road for...?	**Siamo sulla strada giusta per...?**
Fill it up with super, please.	**Per favore, faccia il pieno di super.**
Check the oil/tires/battery.	**Controlli l'olio/le gomme/ la batteria.**
I've had a breakdown.	**Ho avuto un guasto.**
There's been an accident.	**C'è stato un incidente.**

E **ELECTRIC CURRENT** *(elettricità)*. In Sicily you will usually find 220-volt current, but some areas still have 110–130. The voltage is generally indicated on the sockets in hotels but it's best to ask to avoid ruining your shaver or hairdryer.

What's the voltage?	**Qual è il voltaggio?**

EMERGENCIES *(emergenza)*. Depending on the nature of the problem, refer to separate Blueprint entries such as CONSULATES, DRIVING and MEDICAL CARE.

All-purpose emergency number (fire, ambulance, theft) 113
Assistance on the road 116

114

mergency medical services

grigento	2 03 44	Palermo	32 18 60
altanissetta	2 14 66	Ragusa	2 14 10
atania	37 00 00	Syracuse	6 85 55
nna	2 19 33	Trapani	6 29 44
lessina	29 26 66 15		

areful	**Attento**	Police	**Polizia**
ire	**Incendio**	Stop	**Stop**
lelp	**Aiuto**	Stop thief	**Al ladro**

ERRIES and BOAT SERVICES*. You can put your car on a ferry at
enoa (a 22-hour trip) or Livorno (18 hours) for Palermo. Another
talian ferry company leaves every night from Naples for Palermo (9
ours) and once a week for Catania (14 hours) and Syracuse (19 hours).
erries run at frequent intervals from Villa San Giovanni and Reggio
i Calabria to Messina and several times a week from Reggio to Cata-
ia and Syracuse. Hydrofoil crossings between Messina and Reggio
ake 15 minutes but carry passengers only. The hydrofoil between
Iaples and Palermo links the two towns in 5 hours, with a stop at the
sland of Ustica; daily service, except on Tuesdays.

Important: If you're going by car or if you want a cabin, reserve long
oat trips before leaving home, above all in high season (June to
eptember). There's a 50 per cent discount on car ferries (reimbursed
y the company upon return) if you stay at your destination at least six
ays and have foreign licence plates.

To the Aeolian Islands: Hydrofoil services link Messina, Milazzo,
efalù and Palermo to the Aeolian Islands (some of these services may
ot be available in low season), and steamships leave Milazzo and
Iessina daily for Vulcano and Lipari.

There's an overnight ferry from Naples which calls at Stromboli,
anarea, Salina and Lipari on its way to Messina. For reservations:
zienda Autonoma del Turismo, Corso V. Emanuele, 239, Lipari
genzia Carlo Genovese, Via de Pretis, 78, Naples.

GUIDES and INTERPRETERS (*guida; interprete*). Your hotel can
ecommend sightseeing guides who speak your language. There are also
ocal guides near most of the major tourist attractions, but settle on the
rice in advance. Many of the cathedrals in Sicily have coin-operated
aped commentaries.

H

HAIRDRESSERS'*. Italian barbers *(barbiere)* and hairdressers *(parrucchiere)* are justly renowned and their prices are reasonable. Rates are slightly higher in Palermo, Catania and Taormina than in smaller towns. Men can usually find an empty chair without much of a wait, but it's better for women to make an appointment. Hairdressers often have facilities for facial massages and make-up. It is customary to tip the barber 15 per cent of the bill; women should tip the shampooer, manicurist or stylist 15 per cent also.

haircut	**taglio di capelli**
shave	**rasatura**
shampoo and set	**shampo e messa in piega**
rinse	**riflesso**
a colour chart	**la tabella dei colori**
Not too much off (here).	**Non troppo corti (qui).**
A little more off (here).	**Un po' di più (qui).**

HITCH-HIKING *(autostop).* Hitch-hiking is common in Sicily, especially in the summer. Signs forbid the practice at the entrance to *autostrade*; it's best to travel before dark and, if possible, in pairs.

Can you give me a lift to…?   **Può darmi un passaggio fino a…?**

HOTELS and ACCOMMODATION* *(albergo; alloggio).* Sicilian hotels range from five-star de luxe to modest boarding houses *(pensione).* During the tourist season, you should book in advance, but you can invariably find something, even at the last minute, with the assistance of the local tourist office. This office can also provide you with a catalogue listing prices and types of accommodation. Some establishments insist that you take all your meals on the premises.

Convents and monasteries accept overnight visitors and offer comfortable rooms as well as meals. There are quite a few in Catania and Palermo; their addresses can be obtained from the tourist office.

Student hostels *(casa dello studente)* exist in several Sicilian towns—Catania, Messina and Palermo—and are aimed at making cheap accommodation available to students (a student card or other identification is necessary).

Youth hostels *(ostello per la gioventù)* are open to holders of membership cards issued by the A.I.G. *(Associazione Italiana Alberghi per la Gioventù),* the Italian Youth Hostels Association, or by the International Youth Hostel Federation. In Syracuse there's a private youth ostel open all year; the tourist office has the details. Other hostels, both members of the A.I.G.:

Castroreale (Messina): Ostello delle Aquile-Salita Federico d'Aragona, open from June to end of September.

Lipari (Aeolian Islands): Ostello Lipari, Via Castello, 17; tel. (090) 11540. Open from March to end of October.

For information and reservations write to:

Associazione Italiana Alberghi per la Gioventù, Piazza della Republica, 47, Rome; tel. (06) 5913702 or 5913758.

a double/single room with/without bath	**una camera matrimoniale/singola con/senza bagno**
What's the rate per night?	**Qual è il prezzo per una notte?**

HOURS. Sicilians take their siesta period seriously, and just about everything shuts down from 1 to 4 p.m. (or even longer in the heat of the summer). Only restaurants and cafés remain open at this time. The best thing to do is take a long lunch, a nap and adapt to the Mediterranean rhythm of life.

Most state museums open from 9 a.m. to 2 p.m. on weekdays, 9 a.m. to 1 p.m. on Sundays and holidays (some from 10 a.m. to 4 p.m.) and close on Mondays. It's advisable to check with your hotel receptionist before setting out.

Excavations and archaeological sites are usually open from 9 a.m. until an hour or two before sunset (many are closed on Mondays).

Banks do business from 8.30 a.m. to 1.30 p.m., Mondays to Fridays, except holidays. Exchange offices normally reopen after the siesta in late afternoon and are open on Saturdays, at least in the morning. They usually operate on Sundays as well at the airports.

LANGUAGE. Most hotels in Sicily have personnel who speak at least a smattering of English, French or German. Similarly, most shopkeepers can understand enough in other languages to do business. In the interior of Sicily, however, you're less likely to find anything besides Sicilian dialect or Italian.

The Berlitz phrase book ITALIAN FOR TRAVELLERS covers all situations you're likely to encounter, and the new Berlitz Italian-English/English-Italian pocket dictionary contains a 12,500-word glossary of terms and concepts plus a menu-reader supplement.

Do you speak English?	**Parla inglese?**
I don't speak Italian.	**Non parlo l'italiano.**

L **LAUNDRY and DRY CLEANING*** *(lavanderia; tintoria).* In every Sicilian city you'll find launderettes where you can do your laundry yourself or, for a slight extra charge, leave it with an attendant. Some also handle dry cleaning. Otherwise take your dry cleaning to a *tintoria* where you can choose between normal and rapid service. Hotels, too, handle your laundry often with same-day service, but of course at higher rates.

When will it be ready?	**Quando sarà pronto?**
I must have this for tomorrow morning.	**Mi serve per domani mattina.**

M **MAPS.** You can find a wide range of maps of Sicily at news-stands and book shops. The provincial tourist offices also have colourful maps of the island with special emphasis on archaeological sites or gastronomy. When buying road maps, look for the date to be sure you get a recent one. The Touring Club Italiano and the Automobile Club d'Italia sell very good road maps; Falk-Verlag, who provided the maps for this book, also publish maps of Sicily and Italy.

a street plan of…	**una piantina di…**
a road map of…	**una carta stradale di…**

MEDICAL CARE. If your health insurance does not honour bills from foreign countries, you can take out a special short-term policy for your trip. Visitors from Great Britain have the right to claim public health services available to Italians since both countries are members of the E.E.C. Before leaving home get a copy of the Form No. E111 from the Department of Health and Social Security.

If you're in need of medical care, it's best to ask your hotel receptionist to help you find a doctor (or dentist) who speaks English.

The first-aid *(pronto soccorso)* section of municipal hospitals can handle medical emergencies satisfactorily. Call 113 for an ambulance. See also EMERGENCIES.

The Italian *farmacia* (drugstore; chemist's) is open during shopping hours and in each city or section of major urban areas one operates at night and on weekends. The opening schedule for off-hours is posted on every pharmacy door and in the local papers.

a doctor	**un medico**
the hospital	**l'ospedale**
an upset stomach	**il mal di stomaco**
a fever	**una febbre**
a dentist/a toothache	**un dentista/il mal di denti**

MEETING PEOPLE. Sicilians, like other Italians, observe certain formal courtesies. For instance, when you enter a shop or office, or even taxi, the usual greeting is *buon giorno* (good day) or after the siesta, *buona sera* (good evening). When asking someone a question, it's polite to preface it with *per favore* (please), and always remember the *grazie* (thanks) to which one responds *prego* (you're welcome).

Introductions are usually accompanied by handshaking and the phrase *piacere* (it's a pleasure). With people you know well, *ciao* is the casual form of greeting or farewell. The best way to address a waiter or waitress is by saying *senta* which means literally "listen" and used to attract their attention.

MONEY MATTERS. The *lira* (plural *lire*, abbreviated *L.* or *Lit.*) is Italy's monetary unit. Coins include 10-, 50-, 100- and 200-lire pieces; banknotes come in denominations of 500, 1,000, 2,000, 5,000, 10,000, 20,000, 50,000 and 100,000 lire. Italy has issued new 10,000 and 20,000 lire banknotes which look very much alike, so pay attention to the denomination of your currency during all transactions.

There is a shortage of small change in Italy and shopkeepers sometimes give special banknotes called *assegno al portatore*, sweets or postage stamps as change.

You will find the prices in Sicily lower than those in Rome or Milan, specially when you stick to local products.

Credit cards *(carta di credito)*: Most hotels in Sicily and some of the bigger city restaurants and shops accept credit cards. In hiring a car the deposit is waived if you have a recognized card.

Traveller's cheques *(assegno per viaggiatori)* are accepted almost everywhere, but you'd be better off cashing them in the bank or at a currency exchange office rather than in a shop or a hotel where the rates are definitely lower. A passport is required when cashing traveller's cheques.

Currency exchange offices *(cambio)* offer a slightly better rate than banks, but your hotel will give you the lowest rate of all. Passports are usually required when changing money. See also HOURS.

Will you take a traveller's cheque/credit card?	**Accetta un assegno per viaggiatori/una carta di credito?**
I want to change some pounds/dollars.	**Vorrei cambiare delle sterline/dei dollari.**

M **MOPED HIRE** * *(noleggio motocicli)*. Moped and bicycle rental is very limited in Sicily. You can ask at your hotel, camping site or E.P.T. office or look under "Motonoleggio" in the phone book to rent a moped. In Taormina, however, there is one recognized rental agency:

Autorimessa California, Via Bagnoli Croci, 86, tel. 0942/23769.

N **NEWSPAPERS and MAGAZINES** *(giornale; rivista)*. News-stands which sell major European publications are few and far between. Usually, the main tourist centres like Palermo, Taormina and Catania will have a news-stand either in the centre of town or at the airport that carries some foreign papers or magazines. But don't count on regular service unless you make special arrangements.

Have you any English-language newspapers/magazines?	**Avete giornali/riviste in inglese?**

P **PHOTOGRAPHY.** Sicily offers the amateur photographer a splendid spectrum of striking views and dramatic backdrops for snapshots. You can usually take photos with normal flash inside churches and museums, but inquire first. Almost every type and brand of film is on sale in Sicily, but it's probably best to have your film developed and printed when you get home.

I'd like a film for this camera.	**Vorrei una pellicola per questa macchina.**
a black-and-white film	**una pellicola in bianco e nero**
a film for colour prints	**una pellicola per fotografie a colori**
a colour-slide film	**una pellicola di diapositive**
35-mm film	**una pellicola trentacinque millimetri**
super-8	**super otto**

POLICE *(polizia, carabinieri)*. There are several types of police in Italy, and it may be difficult to know which roles each assumes; there's the local city police, who mostly handle traffic, the highway police, and the *carabinieri*, a division of the army. In Sicily, each small town has its unit of *carabinieri*. They are courteous and try to be helpful, though most of them do not, of course, speak foreign languages. But if you call the police switchboard you can often get someone on the phone who may speak English or French.

The all-purpose emergency number is 113.

UBLIC HOLIDAYS *(festa)*. Italy used to have an abundance of ublic and religious holidays but the number has recently been reduced. On the other hand, when a big national holiday falls on a Tuesday or Thursday, you might find that Italians take a *ponte* (bridge) to the weekend, so that some places of business take a day off on Monday or Friday as well.

Banks, government offices, most shops and some museums close on holidays. And during *Ferragosto* almost everything is closed for the whole week, except hotels and those shops and restaurants catering for tourists.

January 1	*Capodanno* or *Primo dell'Anno*	New Year's Day
April 25	*Festa della Liberazione*	Liberation Day
May 1	*Festa del Lavoro*	Labour Day (May Day)
June 29	*Ss. Pietro e Paolo*	Saints Peter and Paul Day
August 15	*Ferragosto*	Assumption Day
November 1	*Ognissanti*	All Saints' Day
December 8	*Immacolata Concezione*	Immaculate Conception
December 25	*Natale*	Christmas Day
December 26	*Santo Stefano*	St. Stephen's Day
Movable Date	*Lunedì di Pasqua (Pasquetta)*	Easter Monday

RELIGIOUS SERVICES. In Catholic churches mass is said daily, and several times on Sundays. Some of the larger Sicilian cities have non-Catholic services which you'll find listed under "Chiese e templi di altri culti" in the yellow pages of the phone book. Following are churches with Protestant services in English:

Palermo: Holy Cross Church, Via M. Stabile, tel. (091) 33 25 57.

Taormina: St. George's Anglican, Via Luigi Pirandello.

What time is mass/the service?   **A che ora è la messa/la funzione?**
Is it in English?   **È in inglese?**

TAXIS* *(tassì* or *taxi)*. It's difficult to find taxis which have meters (especially in Catania) so you should always establish the fare in advance. Because of the constantly rising price of fuel, there is usually

T a *supplemento* added to the metered price and an extra charge is also made for night, Sunday and holiday trips, luggage and certain airport trips. You can check with the hotel or tourist office on the current prices and supplementary charges. A tip of 15 per cent is customary.

Horse-cabs (*carrozza*): A colourful sight for centuries in Sicily, these cabs (usually drawn by donkeys) are rapidly giving way to the internal combustion engine. They still may be found in the Palermo gardens, in Taormina and Catania, and even in remote places like Segesta, where you can pose for a picture in one. The cabs tend to be more expensive than less exotic means of transport so settle on a price in advance.

What's the fare to…? **Qual è la tariffa per…?**

THEFT (*furto*). Petty theft is increasing and the wise tourist will be cautious. If you are robbed, you should contact the police—for insurance purposes if nothing else. Don't sling your handbag over your street-side shoulder, it could be torn off by thieves (*scippatori*) on motorbikes or in cars.

Deposit your documents and unneeded cash in your hotel's safe. Don't display your wallet or money ostentatiously; don't leave valuable coats or bags casually draped over a nearby chair in a restaurant.

Never keep anything of value in your car. It is even unwise to leave your luggage in the trunk of an unattended car, particularly in urban areas; and be careful about leaving your car with just any "attendant".

TIME DIFFERENCES. The following chart shows the difference in time between Sicily and some selected cities, but for a short period during spring and fall when the shift to and from summer time occurs, the difference could be one hour off.

Los Angeles	Chicago	New York	London	**Sicily**
11 a.m.	1 p.m.	2 p.m.	7 p.m.	**8 p.m.**

TOILETS (*gabinetti*). You'll find public toilets in most museums and galleries; restaurants, bars, cafés and large stores are all required to have facilities, as are airports and train stations. You'll also find toilets at gas stations along the motorways. They may be designated in different ways: W.C. (for water closet) with the picture of a man or oman; sometimes the wording will be in Italian—*Uomini* (men) or *onne* (women). The most confusing label for foreigners is *Signori* men—with a final *i*) and *Signore* (women—with a final *e*).

/here are the toilets? **Dove sono i gabinetti?**

OURIST INFORMATION OFFICES. The Italian State Tourist ffices (*Ente Nazionale Italiano per il Turismo*, abbreviated E.N.I.T.) re found in Italy and abroad. They publish detailed brochures with p-to-date information on accommodation, means of transport and her general tips and useful addresses all over Italy.

The Provincial Tourist Boards (*Ente Provinciale per il Turismo*, bbreviated E.P.T.), located in each major town in Italy, offer infor-ation on accommodation, camping and regional events.

In addition, there are strictly local tourist boards and offices (*Azienda utonoma di Soggiorno, Cura e Turismo*) run by municipal authorities. hey provide detailed information on the town's attractions, especially bout opening hours and accommodation. Following are the addresses f main tourist information offices in Italy and abroad:

alian State Tourist Offices

'anada: 3, Place Ville-Marie, Suite 22, Montreal 13, P.Q., tel. (514) 66-76 67

ire: 47 Merrion Square, Dublin 2, tel. 766-397

Jnited Kingdom: 201 Regent Street, London W1R 8AY, tel. (01) 39 23 11

J.S.A.: 500 N. Michigan Avenue, Chicago IL 60601, tel (312) 22-10 83

30 Fifth Avenue, New York, N.Y. 10020, tel. (212) 245-48 22

. Francis Hotel, Post Street, San Francisco, CA 94108, tel. (415) 92-62 07

aly: At the Italian border crossings and in the port arrival offices in enoa and Naples, you may get the pamphlets mentioned above, as ell as Italian Touring Club brochures and maps.

'rovincial Tourist Boards, Sicily

atania: Largo Paisiello, 5; tel. (095) 31 21 24/31 64 07

1essina: Stazione F.S.; tel. (090) 77 53 35

'alermo: Piazza Castelnuovo, 35; tel. (091) 58 38 47/24 50 80

eroporto di Punta Raisi; tel. (091) 28 19 86

yracuse: Corso Gelone, 92-c; tel. (0931) 6 76 07

T The E.P.T. offices are usually open from 9.30 to 11.30 a.m., although those at the Punta Raisi and Fontanarossa Airports operate from 8 a.m. to late afternoon with only a break around 2 or 3 p.m. for a couple of hours.

TRAINS* *(treno).* The Italian State Railways (*Ferrovie dello Stato* or *F.S.*) in Sicily has an efficient rail network. In the better-class trains there are dining cars, or you can be served at your seat. If you haven't booked a seat in advance be sure to get to the station at least a half hour before departure time, as trains are usually crowded. Although for certain trips the inter-city buses are much faster, for others the train might better serve your purpose. For example, from Taormina to Syracuse by *Rapido* takes just over an hour and a half (by *Accelerato* an hour longer). The following chart explains the different types of Italian trains:

Rapido: non-stop between largest towns. Seat reservations are essential; a supplement of 25 per cent is charged. The best of these for Sicily is the *Peloritano* which runs between Rome and Palermo, Syracuse and Catania.

Direttissimo: stops once or twice between towns. Both first and second class (you can reserve seats in first-class carriages).

Diretto: These slower trains stop more frequently, even unpredictably, at most stations.

Accelerato or *Locale:* a train that stops for a long time at every station.

There are fare reductions such as the *Biglietti turistici di libera circolazione* or "travel-at-will" tickets suitable for tourists who intend to travel in Italy extensively (only available *outside* the Italian borders). They are good for various periods (8, 15, 21 and 30 days). Children between 4 and 12 pay half on all fares.

One interesting train ride is around Mount Etna on the *Ferrovia Circumetnea;* the 144-kilometre trip lasts about 5 hours. You take the main line from Catania to Giarre-Riposto to connect with the Circumetnea line.

When does the train for... leave?	**Quando parte il treno per...?**
I'd like to make seat reservations.	**Vorrei riservare dei posti.**

...gle (one-way)	**andata**
...turn (round-trip)	**andata e ritorno**
...rst/second class	**prima/seconda classe**
...eeping car	**vagone letto**
...ning car	**vagone ristorante**
...uchette	**cuccette**

...ATER *(acqua).* You don't need to worry about drinking tap water in ...cily in any respectable hotel. If for some reason water isn't drinkable, ...ere should be a sign reading *acqua non potabile.*
Most Italians, however, out of habit, prefer bottled water, especially ... mealtime, to go along with the wine.

...bottle of mineral water	**una bottiglia di acqua minerale**
...rbonated/non-carbonated	**gasata/naturale**

OME USEFUL EXPRESSIONS

...es/no	**sì/no**
...lease/thank you	**per favore/grazie**
...xcuse me/you're welcome	**mi scusi/prego**
...here/when/how	**dove/quando/come**
...esterday/today/tomorrow	**ieri/oggi/domani**
...ft/right	**sinistra/destra**
...ig/small	**grande/piccolo**
...heap/expensive	**buon mercato/caro**
...pen/closed	**aperto/chiuso**
...don't understand.	**Non capisco.**
...What does this mean?	**Cosa significa?**
...lease write it down.	**Lo scriva, per favore.**
...Vaiter!/Waitress!	**Senta!**
...'d like...	**Vorrei...**
...Iow much is that?	**Quant'è?**

Index

An asterisk (*) next to a page number indicates a map reference.